THE END A LOVE STORY

THE END A LOVE STORY

A MEMOIR BY ELIZABETH SCHLESSMAN BENTSON

TATE PUBLISHING
AND ENTERPRISES, LLC

Published by Tate Publishing & Enterprises, LLC
127 E. Trade Center Terrace | Mustang, Oklahoma 73064 USA
1.888.361.9473 | www.tatepublishing.com

Tate Publishing is committed to excellence in the publishing industry. The company reflects the philosophy established by the founders, based on Psalm 68:11,

"The Lord gave the word and great was the company of those who published it."

Book design copyright © 2016 by Tate Publishing, LLC. All rights reserved.
Cover design by Joana Quilantang
Interior design by Manolito Bastasa

Published in the United States of America

ISBN: 978-1-68207-219-6
Biography & Autobiography / General
15.11.05

In order to get through the sudden crises of my parents' health decline, I was encouraged to keep a journal of whom I talked to and what they said. Thus, this journal became a catharsis for the chaos of the present and a reminiscence of the past. After spending my day at the hospital or after interviewing rehab facilities and assisted living residences, I would pour myself a glass of wine and jot down what I had found and my thoughts. This led to an inner reflection of what my parents' personalities truly were and what paths they had chosen to get to this point in their lives. I took some of their words and their assumed thoughts over the years and started a biography of Walt and Marian and who they really were—rather than today's circumstances of who they had become, or rather what circumstances were making them into today's perception of who they were. They were once real people, with real ideas and a real life, real hopes, real dreams, and real love, and I wanted to remember that for them, while I tried to make decisions to honor them at the close of their lives.

This is what I wrote.

January 2013, 1:30 a.m.

The phone rings, awakening us from sleep.

"Your father is not doing well. We think you should come."

We throw on clothes, hearts beating wildly, but we are strangely calm, as if in a trance. We arrive at the hospital and enter near the emergency entrance, where we have been entering every day for the past week, and take the stairs, not waiting for the elevator. His bed is outside his room in the hall corner. He is surrounded by two nurses and two technicians and some sort of machine.

Before I even get next to Dad, a nurse asks me, "Does he have a DNR?"

I answer that I think so. I say hi to Dad who is struggling to breathe, and I start massaging his shoulder, telling him to breathe slowly, in and out, like Lamaze, in and out, in and out, in and out. I think they have given him a shot of something and he is calming down—or maybe it's because we are here. It's a long hour, in and out, in and out, in and out, but I think he wants to live, he's not ready to quit, he's such a strong person—he's a fighter.

He wasn't always Bapa. He started out as Walter, then became Walt, Honey, Daddy, Grampa, and then Bapa, because that's what his young grandson could say easily.

She wasn't always Marian. She was Mimsey to her sister and the Queen of the May. She went to school, went off to college, went back home as World War II started, and then she evolved into the independent Marian—wife, mother, grandmother, great-grandmother, and then, lost soul.

"Was it Bubbles who introduced us?" she asked.

"Yes, it was. I asked her out but she said she was busy. However, she said she had a friend who worked on base for the Director of OSS, so I went over and checked you out," he replied.

"Oh. I thought the date was set. I didn't know you checked me out!"

Six months later they were married. It was wartime. Things moved fast. Then the Powers that be decided to close the Army Air Force base in Casper.

"We're transferred to Albuquerque," he announced one day.

"Great," she said. "I love the warmth."

DAD

Saturday, January 5th

"Hey, wake up sleepyhead. It's time to head to the Base for groceries."

I had arrived at Mom and Dad's house to take them grocery shopping, trying to get Dad to not drive any more but without saying anything. He seemed to be OK with our doing more and more, but today he was still in bed.

"I'm not feeling too well, so don't think I want to go to the base (cough, cough)."

"OK, we'll just head over to Rouse's and pick up a few staples, then fix your dinner."

Sunday, January 6th

I arrive to take him to church. Tammy, whom we've had helping for several months, had been there earlier and gotten Mom ready for the day and fixed Dad's breakfast, then put it in the refrigerator—cereal with bananas and apple-sauce. The coffee was ready to go, his cup set out. Dad was still in bed having a hard time catching his breath. I was beginning to fear pneumonia so I raised his upper body with pillows and he was wheezing less.

"Go on without me, I'm just not up to par," he said.

Michael came over in the afternoon and we agreed that Dad should get to the doctor's office first thing Monday morning.

Monday, January 7th

A flu epidemic was in full force in the South, and maybe the US. Although Mom and Dad had gotten their flu shots a month ago, Dad tested positive for the flu.

The doctor said, "You can either go home or go to the hospital. Things can happen really fast with a person your age and with this flu. It's your choice where you choose to get well."

"I think I want to go to the hospital," my dad replied.

Everyone had donned a mask at this point as he was contagious, then Michael drove him to Northshore Hospital, where I met them and got him checked in. I called my brother and arranged to have him fly in and help. Then I went and got Mom to spend the night at my house.

———■◆■———

The lights are on, it's dark outside, Mom is roaming the halls. She can't find her bed. I lead her back to bed.

Another hour has passed. It's 2 a.m., the lights are on. Mom is in another bed. I turn on the bathroom light and leave her in the new bed.

A form is wandering into our bedroom. It's Mom, searching for her bed. I lead her back. Worried that she'll fall down the stairs, I take my pillow out to the hall to sleep a few hours, guarding the stairs.

Tuesday, January 8th

Michael and I visit Dad on our way to pick up my brother Alan at the airport. Mom stays in the car and I head upstairs at the hospital. Dad is in an isolation room, as this flu is contagious. I figure I've been exposed quite well by now, so just ignore donning the mask. We think this is a respiratory flu as he's having a hard time breathing. They are going to take another x-ray; we're all worried about pneumonia.

Wednesday, January 9th

Alan leaves Mom at the house in Diamondhead, as she is used to staying by herself when Dad goes to golf or to the doctor.

"It's been an interesting night," Alan says, as Mom wandered some, so he finally just shut his door.

Dad is still in isolation and glad to see Alan, who dons a mask since he hasn't been around the flu-persons for the last week as we have. We hang around the hospital waiting to talk to a doctor. They have a new system now where you have a hospital doctor to take care of you, not your regular one, plus your specialist if you have one, which Dad has. Two, in fact—a cardiologist and a nephrologist. They get to do the balancing act of keeping his heart going so that his kidneys function, so that the fluid doesn't build up around his heart, so that it can continue to function. It is a fine balancing act. Dad's legs are puffing up, as they do when he retains fluid. Then they will blister and weep. We've been down this road before but he always does OK. It just takes time.

Thursday, January 10th

They're moving Dad down the hall to a private room. The staff is beginning to look familiar, and Dad jokes a little with everyone. The oxygen and breathing treatments are helping and he seems to be recovering from the flu.

Friday, January 11th, to Sunday, January 13th

All hell has broken loose. Alan, Michael, and I take turns being with Dad at the hospital or Mom at home. Dad has been doing OK but is no longer able to get out of bed and walk alone. Saturday we meet with the nephrologist, who says we have three choices for Dad:

1. dialysis,
2. continue on drugs to see how much the kidneys can take, or
3. hospice.

That hasn't even been a thought, he just has the flu! He was driving and at the casino last week. I break down. We are crushed.

Mom can't live on her own so now we wonder not only about their survival but where, and with whom, and under what circumstances. What a difference a week makes. Mom has gotten lost twice this last week but doesn't know it. She was banging on the neighbor's door thinking it was her house and was belligerent when she was redirected to her own house. Alan heard her banging on the neighbor's back door and by the time he got there another neighbor had come over to escort Mom home. This hasn't happened before, but she must have gotten confused while picking up leaves in the driveway and she turned back down the adjacent driveway. She's going to spend mornings at the beauty shop with Tammy to give Alan some respite. She can putter around, but there will be lots of eyes on her as she roams.

Monday, January 14th

They want to release Dad as he is now over the flu. That's why he was in the hospital and now they've cured it. But he is too weak to walk, or even get out of bed on his own. They still want him out of the hospital and suggest a physical therapy/rehab program, so Alan and I will visit our three local choices. Think we should also visit some assisted living places for later, or hire Tammy full time to live with Mom and Dad. What will be best for them? Dad is confused about what is happening, as are we.

Tuesday, January 15th

Oh my God! What horrible, depressing places the rehab facilities are. The staff is nice enough, but the residents are so incomprehensible. The neurological one is so depressing, and we toured the "good" wing. The building is getting a facelift, so the walls are freshly painted and it does have some décor, but the inhabitants are sleeping in wheelchairs out in the halls with tubes in them, or in beds with ventilators, or they are paralyzed and moaning. Nothing is encouraging, so Alan and I head to the next place and encounter a mad woman in a wheelchair screaming profanities. This lasts a little too long before she is pushed back to her room to rant. Unfortunately, this is the place we choose as it is closest geographically to us, and is the least offensive. Hopefully, it will just be a week before Dad gets his strength back and can get home.

And so it has come to this...

Albuquerque was great, but brief. Dad was soon sent to Wichita to replace a bombardier who had come down with appendicitis. Mom packed up, drove to Wichita to say good-bye temporarily as Dad left for California with the squadron and then the Pacific corridor, island hopping from Tinian to Guadjalein to Okinawa. A few days after the atomic bombs were dropped, he flew over Japan and then over the USS *Missouri* to witness the signing of the Japanese surrender and the end of the war. It was six months later before he could return to the States.

Mom, meanwhile, had returned to Casper and was living with her mom and dad. Her mom had put out feelers and found a neighborhood grocery store that was up for sale, the Grant Street Grocery. She and Dad became partners and purchased it. Dad learned to cut meat, make hamburger, stock shelves, fix compressors before the frozen food melted, and have coffee and doughnuts with the neighborhood ladies at 8 a.m. The store soon gained a reputation for the best meat in town and the friendliest butcher. The hunters brought in their bucks and the cattlemen brought in their 4-H meat for Dad to prepare and package. Mom baked lasagna and lemon meringue pies to sell at the store.

At the end of each month, the home mangle became mom's desk as she did the billing for the few charge customers. Soon I came along, followed by my brother Alan. Mom and Dad bought a new three-bedroom house on a hill just a few blocks from the grade school. It had large beamed ceilings and floor-to-ceiling windows along the back to let the sunshine in. Dad built a fence around the backyard and Mom started growing her wonderful flower and vegetable gardens. She would stroll around the yard teaching Alan and me all the names of the flowers and trees, and we would help pick green beans and tomatoes for dinner, or we would just lie in the grass and watch the clouds, discussing what animals they looked like.

Grant Street Grocery
Early Family

DAD

Heritage Manor of Slidell
The care plan conference for Mr. Schlessman
is scheduled for 1-31-13 @ 1:15 am/pm
The care plan meetings are time sensitive in
an effort to ensure that families are not kept
waiting. Going forward, state regulations now
requires (sic) that all residents have on file a copy
of a PHYSICIAN ORDER FOR SCOPE OF
TREATMENT (DNR or FULL CODE).

Wednesday, January 16th

Heritage Manor check-in at 5:30 p.m. A van transports him
from the hospital. He eats dinner in the dining room in a
wheelchair, then is wheeled to his bed by Alan and Michael.

Thursday, January 17th

11 a.m. Nothing happening. I then talked with Patrick and Stacy (administrators), then met with Hannah (speech therapist) and Lori (occupational therapist). I pointed out the dirty dresser and stressed not letting Dad languish.

2 p.m. I checked and got good reports. Andrew said he walked fifteen steps.

Friday, January 18th

8:15 a.m. I found him in the dining room in a wheelchair, eating breakfast.

8:40 a.m. Just us in the dining room. No one has come to get him, so I hailed Patrick to voice concern again. Dad has not had a bath, has an ankle wound, and was ignored. An assistant comes to take him to a bath.

12:30 p.m. Michael found him with Hannah in the dining room, shaved and showered and doing well. He had done some occupational therapy with his arms and felt good; breathing therapy also performed.

4:30 p.m. He is in the room napping, his left arm wrapped. He had walked some, and we're regaining hope that he can do this. He's tired.

MOM

"I think Mom and Dad would be comfortable here," I say to my brother as we are out touring assisted living centers. "This one, Memory Lane, is fairly close to my office, near their bridge center, has high ceilings and has a homey feel about it."

"Yes," Alan responds, "I think Dad would enjoy the poker night and Friday afternoon Happy Hour."

"We'll get it all set up for them so he can come here and do some therapy after he gets out of rehab. Even if he can't walk much, then the halls are wide enough for his Rollator. Denny, Kelly, and the girls are coming in this weekend and can help us move their furniture in and get Mom settled. I know Dad has been against this and said it would be the bitter end when he moved into assisted living, but I just don't see how they can manage by themselves anymore. We could move them home and have Tammy come in more, but Dad is going to need someone full time for a while. This way he can try out assisted living but with the option of going home if he prefers," I say, trying to talk us both into the next phase of Mom and Dad's life.

Thursday, January 17th

We moved in a twin bed from our house to Memory Lane. It was one of her childhood Jenny Lind beds which I had been using in the guest room and which my kids had slept on during childhood. I took an air mattress for myself to sleep on as I planned on spending the first few nights with her to get her acclimated to the Memory part of assisted living.

8:30 p.m. Mom is in bed, I am in the living room of her apartment on the air mattress.

Friday, January 18th

An aide checked around 3 a.m. to see if Mom needed to use the bathroom.

5 a.m. Mom was up and looking for the bathroom. She turned out the lights and was disoriented, so I directed her back to bed.

6:30 a.m. Back to the bathroom via the closet (no lights on) and she wanted to stay up, but I put her back in bed.

7 a.m. The aide checked to see if she was ready to get dressed, but I declined for her, as she was back asleep.

7:30 a.m. She was up and cold, so we dressed her and got ready for the day.

8 a.m. Victoria, a more senior aide, came to meet Mom and took her to the dining room for group breakfast. I gave Victoria a notecard where all Mom's family would be in case she asked, and I headed home for a rest.

12:30 p.m. I found Mom in the dining room finishing lunch; notes by the aide and Victoria indicated that Mom ate breakfast and lunch, did some exercise (which she usually abhors!) and participated in activities. She was happy, not anxious, so I left.

Saturday, January 19th

I found Mom in the dining room—no teeth, no hearing aids, and in Depends. I took her to her apartment and changed all that, then got her in the car and went to see Daddy at the rehab center for their Wine & Cheese Social. Our son, Denny, and his wife Kelly and their two little girls Addie and Kiki had made it into town and were going to help Michael move some furniture from Mom and Dad's house to Memory Lane and finish getting Mom settled.

DAD

Saturday, January 19th

We walk in and he was facing the wall. He had gone to breakfast, brought himself back to the room, and was dozing in his wheelchair. Nicky changed him and there was a smell; she said he was drenched. Someone should have changed him before her shift, apparently.

We bring Mom over in the afternoon for the Social Wine & Cheese. Dad's not there. I go to his room and wake him up.

"Mom's at the Wine & Cheese Social. She's waiting for you," I announce.

We get Dad into the wheelchair and take him to the social. Mom smiles when she sees him, then notices he's in a wheelchair.

"What happened to you?" she asks.

"I've been sick, the flu," he says.

Dad beams at her, not saying anything more, just smiling. They drink their wine and have a cookie.

"What happened to you?" Mom asks again.

"I've been sick," Dad replies.

Later that evening, we swing by Dad's on our way out to dinner in order to check on him, as I think he might be sad and missing Mom. He's seated in his wheelchair in the back of a group watching a movie. He smiles when he sees Addie and Kiki and reaches out to hold hands with them.

Sunday, January 20th

Michael and Denny arrived at 9 a.m. He was eating in bed (yogurt with strawberries). They get him out of bed and into a wheelchair.

Later that day, after going to a Mardi Gras parade in town, Addie and Kiki want to take him some beads they caught at the parade. Nicky is on duty. Dad has had good bathroom habits so far. We played catch in the hall, then wheeled him down to watch the game, racing his wheelchair against Kiki, Addie, and myself. We watch the San Francisco playoff game, then head to dinner. When we return, he is ready for bed. Not a lot of activity that evening.

Monday, January 21st (MLK Day)

Denny and Kelly go to see Bapa at 8:30 a.m. Brittany, an aide on duty, has an attitude going. Dad had been in the dining room, rounding the corner in his wheelchair by himself, and has been waiting for Brittany to give him his medications. Brittany wanted to put him in his room, which was dark because the blinds weren't raised. Barbara, the resident ombudsman, said Dad has rights. We mention to Brittany about Sittercise, the exercise group he's supposed to be in, she said she would take care of it. Bathroom is done with a different aide. Kelly and Denny told Brittany they were taking Bapa to Sittercise. She objected, but when they got to the Sittercise group, they were the last ones there.

Michael and I visit at 7 p.m. Hannah met us at the door with good news about his swallowing—small bites, small sips—and relayed that the physical therapist said Bapa did really well walking with a walker. He has some bleeding and edema but the wound woman is doing well with him. I told him he was doing great. Kelly and I had gone to Diamondhead and cleaned out the refrigerator. I told him it was like going to Grant Street Grocery. We started him thinking about what to do on his anniversary; think he had a positive attitude and looked good. Nicky is the night nurse, so all will be good. She's on the same game plan as we are.

Tuesday, January 22nd

Michael joins Dad for breakfast, then returns to our house.

Surprise! While Michael is at home, Dad is taken to the ER as he has a new cut on his left leg that starts bleeding more when his bandage is taken off for showering. We find him in the ER, shivering and wrapped in towels. I hug him and rub his back. Turns out he needs inner and outer stitches. They take an x-ray of his left arm because of the pain and swelling—edema and arthritis. Back to Heritage for a late lunch. I sit with him. They had kept his plate warm.

What is going on?

MOM

Sunday, January 20th

I noticed discharge in Mom's eyes. An aide says Mom needs socks and underpants, so Kelly labels the dresser drawers on the outside as to their contents and puts up signs saying NO DEPENDS. We have good interaction with Mom, although it seems like she has digressed.

Monday, January 21st

Denny goes over to Mom's at 10:30. Mom is tossing a ball in a group and doesn't want to leave the game. After she has lunch, Denny brings her to my house before taking her to the doctor for the eye and cough issues. She is a little disoriented. Doctor's appointment confirms pinkeye and congestion—no flu, thank God. Kelly and I hang pictures and drapes at Mom's apartment, then work a jigsaw puzzle with Mom, give her a Boost and aspirin, then head back to the doctor for the prescription. She brings along a word puzzle book to entertain herself. She seems congenial and happy, although docile and not much spirit or independence. She's lost weight and is shrinking—118 pounds and 5'3".

Tuesday, January 22nd

Kelly visits Mom. She has no teeth nor hearing aids in, her medicine wasn't given to her, she's greasy and unkempt. No one is able to give any information on showering except that it's not on their shift. I call Memory Lane for information on when she gets a shower and shampoo and reiterate that she needs hearing aids and dentures and glasses in the morning, that's who she is. I asked about the eye drops for the pinkeye and am told, "Your mother doesn't like eye drops." I already know that. I pointed out that she needs to be lying down to accept eye drops and would still put up a fuss. Victoria asks how they are expected to do that, to which I respond, "I don't know, you are the professionals. Do I need to come over three times a day to put eye drops in and give her a cough pill?"

Later in the day, I get a call from Memory Lane requesting a meeting as I had been rude. I get in the car and drive over to Memory Lane, but all the people I am to meet with cannot be found, so I go to find Mom. She's asleep in the dining room. I awaken her, take her to her apartment for eye drops, Claritin, and a cough pill. She's coughing horribly, wobbly and weak. I give her some cranberry juice with the pills. She wants to go to the bathroom, struggles, can't wipe, and when getting redressed she notices that she's wet, so we change pants and undies. She lies on the bed for eye drops. The eyes are getting better but she is still coughing, so I have her sit upright in a chair while she works on a crossword puzzle. I give her a Boost too and then we walk back to dinner in the dining room. All the staff is there, so we go over Mom's routine and I offer apologies as I have been stressed. Two weeks ago I had seminormal parents, people living in their own home. Now we are on a trampoline.

They had a simple wedding—January 23, 1944. It was wartime and winter in Wyoming. His parents came out from Pittsburgh and her parents lived in Wyoming. There was snow but that didn't prevent them from driving to Denver for their honeymoon. And thus they were together every January 23 for sixty-nine years, except for this one.

65TH ANNIVERSARY

Walter and Marian Schlessman celebrated their 65th anniversary at Diamondhead Country Club with their daughter Libby Bentson of Pearl River. The Schlessmans met in Casper, Wyo., where Walter was stationed as an Army Air Corps instructor, and they were married Jan. 23, 1944. After World War II the couple settled in Casper and operated a successful grocery store until 1980, when they relocated to Diamondhead. They are frequent bridge and golf players in Slidell. They also have a son, Alan, in Denver, Colo.; four granchildren; and three great-grandchildren.

DAD

Wednesday, January 23rd

Michael joined Dad for breakfast. He spilled some, but eating went well—small bites and small sips. Kelly joined Bapa for lunch and it was good again. Bapa said he had walked down the hall. He and Kelly set 12 days as a goal. I visited for dinner at 5 p.m. He was sleeping in his wheelchair, in the room, covered with towels as he was cold. I brought his Pitt sweatshirt, so got him into it. He was confused, thought it morning, not dinnertime. I asked if he needed to go to the bathroom before dinner, he said he'd just go in his diaper. I was not happy.

We went to the dining room. I wheeled him in the wheelchair, they were having coffee before dinner, so I got him a confetti cupcake that Kelly and the girls had made for their anniversary. He enjoyed it with coffee (hors d'oeuvres!). We had a strange couple as tablemates, and

Boudreaux introduced himself and admired all the family support. Dad's dinner came: milk, applesauce, and a plate of shredded chicken, peas, rice and gravy. He ate well. He said no to Bingo, so I called Kelly and told her not to come join him. I took him back to the room, he was tired. Nicky was his nurse, said she would help in a few minutes, she was busy delivering dinners. Dad fell asleep several times in the wheelchair. I offered to take him to the bathroom to brush his teeth, but he was too tired (ice treatments on his arm earlier had helped relieve the pain). I woke him up a few times more while in the chair, until Nicky came. I left with instructions to raise his arm. He's come so far in a week, but doesn't know Mom's deteriorating so.

MOM

Wednesday, January 23rd

Addie and I visited Memory Lane. Addie wanted to show me the great game she had played with Mom, but when I got there at 10:30, Mom was on the couch. I asked her to get up several times, then she did and was very shaky and off balance. I took her arm to walk her to the door, and by the time we got to the door to give the security code, she had pulled away. I got the door open and took Mom's arm again, but she pulled away outside the door and grabbed the bench rail to pull herself along, then fell over backward. Three aides came out, but we were really OK. Prima Donna Mom then put her glasses and shoes back on after sitting up and swearing. Another aide came over and asked if I needed help getting her up. I said yes. We got Mom up, she shook me off, said she didn't need help. The aide had her hand on Mom's back holding her. I realized we would not make it back to the room and thought it best to head to the dining room for lunch. We got her seated, and Addie and I went back to the room to get her Claritin. Addie stayed to work on the Audubon puzzle. I went back to the dining room and had Mom take her Claritin to stop her cough. I had my arm around her, but she shrugged it off.

Michael went back in the evening, not sure she really recognized him. She was coughing a lot. She was staring at the TV in the dining room but not understanding it, so he brought her puzzle book to her, turned it to a new page, and started to help her with a puzzle. She made wavy lines on the page. Apparently, she can't do word puzzles any more. She's losing more and more of her intelligence, it seems.

8 p.m. The Walgreens practitioner calls back to check on Mom. He OKs the cough syrup (half a dose) but recommends a doctor follow-up on Friday if the cough isn't better. It could be bronchitis.

Happy Anniversary.

The Cocktail Hour

After fifteen years of marriage and plenty of *Vive la joie!* parties, the predinner cocktail hour emerged. With their two children firmly established in school and piano lessons, life was going well for Walt and Marian. The store was turning a bit of a profit so a bottle of gin or bourbon could be bought each month with no strain on the budget. Dad closed the store Monday through Saturday at 6 p.m., then five to ten minutes to get home and Mom would have a gimlet, martini, or whiskey sour waiting for him. They sat in the living room in front of the TV and watched *I Love Lucy*, sipping their cocktails, not really talking, but just being with each other. Dinner was already cooking on the stove or in the oven: meatloaf, breaded veal cutlets, bologna ring, or one large hamburger patty, with some sort of potato dish, vegetable, and salad. Dessert was in the refrigerator or the oven. Sundays were fried chicken, ham, or rump roast. Dinner was full of conversation of who had come into the store and the pleasantries that were exchanged. We were practicing our "El Salvador" manners as mom's sister and her husband were being sent to San Salvador with the Air Force as military attaché. They would have a big house with servants and entertain a lot, and we would all need to know which fork to use, which direction to pass or receive food, and which glass held water. So night after night for a couple of years we practiced our "El Salvador" manners and learned a little Spanish to be able to be appreciative of the actions of the servants.

Mom had always wanted to travel and see the world. Dad had seen some of it during WWII, so that wanderlust was already implanted and the El Salvador plan was triggering what would become the next part of their life—the travels.

Oh! The travels. Off to see the world, and they did. Mom followed Marco Polo's route and then got caught in the 6 Days War in Egypt. (Michael said she started it!) She fled to the Canadian Embassy in Cairo in the middle of the night with several other travelers to seek refuge, then sent a cable to Dad saying she was all right. We had no idea what was going on so found it a little strange to receive such a cable.

Then Dad, as president of the Lion's Club, was invited to Japan for a convention, so he and Mom went and thoroughly enjoyed Asia. Indulged in Chinese scotch even! Then they found Ports-of-Call and jaunted around the world. There were mystery trips, where they were told only what clothes to bring—a swimsuit, warm weather clothes, cold weather clothes—but always a passport. And they got a badge for each country to add to their nametags so they could remember where they'd been and compare notes with other travelers.

But first we camped. Mom and Dad had little money so Mom invested in a tent, cots, and sleeping bags. In the summer in Wyoming, we would join family friends and camp in an old sheepherder's cabin for the adults, and tents for the kids. Mom always brought a green and white chenille bedspread for her and Dad's bed, and a tablecloth for the camp table. We would be civilized being out in the wild. The ladies would prepare dinner over the potbellied stove in the cabin, while the gentlemen prepped drinks outside and the kids (me and others) set logs around the campfire for seating and roasting marshmallows and singing after dinner. Kum ba yah.

Lots of cocktails among the adults and enthusiasm among the children led to great entertainment around the campfire and into the night where we would hear ghost stories and myths of the Wyoming forests. After a day or two of fishing and celebrating, we would pack up, check our bodies for ticks, and look forward to the next camping trip, probably Labor Day at Jenny Lake in Jackson, another campsite, another camp stove, but plenty of games around the campfire and breakfast of fried fish and hash browns. Beautiful scenery, pleasant stories, and lots of camaraderie.

When Dad and Mom sold the Grant Street Grocery, they wanted to travel more. They collected the money from the receivables and purchased a small motorhome. Oh so much fun! It was a cab-over, and the dining table retracted to form a bed. They first went to Yellowstone, then on to Glacier and Banff. Alan accompanied them on this scenic tour, and all learned how to hook up at a campsite and remove the liquids accumulated during the day. That motorhome transported them all across the USA and on into Alaska, with Mom's "gold" silverware, bedspreads, and tablecloths. Over the years, they upgraded to bigger and better motorhomes, which we all borrowed for grandchildren's swim meets, high school sports events, college tailgating, or all of us bonding at beach and mountain vacations.

Upon graduation of Libby, Michael, and Alan, Mom and Dad thought we needed a world tour (which we did!) so we went to Europe. Landing in Germany, we ventured up to Wolfsburg to purchase "Clementine," a VW squareback, which would transport us around Europe and then be transported to New Orleans. We picked up the car after a lengthy explanation in French (everyone assumed Libby could understand this, since she had a MA in French), and that was the shortest line, then we went to our first castle and were mesmerized. Mom, after all her studies and dreams of Europe, had arranged the perfect trip, the perfect introduction to Europe.

There would be many more, for all of us, as well as she and Dad, but this was exquisite—Germany, Holland, France, Switzerland, Italy, Ireland, and England. What a grand introduction.

Walt and Marian continued their travels to Russia, to India, to South America, to Australia and New Zealand, to Kenya, to everywhere in the world. And they brought back souvenirs, small enough to fit into their home or to be given to their children, but large enough to evoke memories of the trip.

MOM

Saturday, January 26th

Visited Mom after lunch. She was seated in a low chair with everyone else in a circle around the TV. She had trouble getting out of the chair. When she did, she said she smelled and had to go to the bathroom. She had messed in her pants. I went to her room and got clean undies. The aides cleaned her up and she came and sat with us. She didn't want to go out, so I left to get batteries for her hearing aids and cough medicine. Kelly got her to come to her room, where I gave her cranberry juice, aspirin, and Claritin. She sat down and worked the jigsaw puzzle. We had a good afternoon. I took her back to the dining room with a crossword puzzle. She's really declined in mental acuteness and physical strength. She wasn't hungry when we left—"Are you going too?"—and not as anxious.

Sunday, January 27th

Denny and I found Mom in the main room around 2 p.m. She was seated in the circle around the TV and saw us come in. I asked her to get up a few times, to no avail. I asked if she needed to go to the bathroom; the aides said she'd just gone. Denny and I went to her apartment and got Claritin and a cough tablet and a glass of cranberry juice. We went back to her and she took them all. We had also taken a crossword puzzle book to her, and she did look at it rather than stare into space. She talked, but not with a lot of sense. She kept looking at her watch to see what time it was. We said we'd be back for dinner and we left.

Monday, January 28th

Kaitlyn was there to help after Mom crumbled and fell down. I'd picked up my brother at the airport and we stopped by Mom's first. I sent Alan in to see if she recognized him; I think she did. She was huddled under a zebra-striped blanket in the circle around the TV. Kaitlyn says she loves the blanket and thinks it is hers. She made quite a fuss when they tried to take it away from her last night, so they let her take it to her apartment. Alan offered his hand to her, she reached for it, put the zebra blanket aside, and struggled to get up out of the chair. She took my brother's arm and walked a few shaky steps before her knees and strength gave out and she melted onto the floor. I came through the door and knelt beside her, pretending it was a silly happenstance.

"What are you doing here on the floor? Let's get your glasses on and sit here for a moment."

A wheelchair appeared and Kaitlyn suggested she use it. One of the circle ladies said Mom wet her pants when she went down, so let's go get her changed. Mom enjoyed the carriage ride down the hall to her apartment. Kaitlyn cleaned her and picked out new clothes. Then we moved her to her living room to visit and relax, Mom seated in the wheelchair, we on the old familiar couch. Mom looked around, noticed the family collage on the wall and the family Christmas cards on the refrigerator.

"There's my sister, her husband, me, and above…?"

"That's Alan."

"There's a young girl with her mother."

"That's me with Jennifer, a long time ago, at the Two Cent Ranch."

"Merry and Bright."

"Yes, that's the Christmas card from Denny and Kelly. Here we all are—"

"What time is it?"

"It's dinnertime, let's go to dinner."

Tuesday, January 29th

I watched through the door to see if Mom interacted or exercised. She sat and observed. I went in and she smiled. "Hi, Mom." I sat down by her. I watched the aide take each resident for potty time. She got to Mom and Mom said no, she didn't have to go to the bathroom. I asked her to get her up, since she had fallen yesterday with my brother. "Just stand there for a minute and get your bearings," I said. Then we started walking, slowly, with help, but just to the table. The aide said she hadn't been eating much, so I went down to her apartment and got her a Boost, Claritin, aspirin, and Chapstick. We sat at the table. It was Song Time (horribly so), but Mom and I became our own choir, singing "God Bless America" and "Yankee Doodle." I said I was going to get Alan and left. He and I then sang Louis Armstrong's "What a Wonderful World."

Wednesday, January 30th

I didn't go see her, but Alan took her back to her apartment to use the potty and work on a jigsaw puzzle.

Thursday, January 31st

I joined Mom for lunch. Alan was already there visiting her in the circle of Memory Lane. He came over to me and said he'd give her a few minutes as she was lost. I got an update on Dad, where Alan had been earlier, then headed over to Mom. She had a glass of water and said she couldn't leave the circle. They were having an election and she wanted to vote. Wasn't I running for something? She finally got up tentatively when I convinced her we were going to lunch downstairs and she could vote later. She was quite wobbly, and still had her bedroom slippers on, so shuffled along. We went to her room. She allowed me to take her arm and help her along. Her lips were very chapped. We got to the room which had her name on the door, but she didn't recognize it. She sat at the table and eyed the jigsaw puzzle which we had been working on. I got her a little Boost, aspirin, and Claritin, plus some cranberry juice on ice. It was very "hot"—cold did not come into her mind. We talked a little more and she started making more sense. Got shoes and knee highs on her. We went into the bathroom to brush her teeth as her breath was atrocious. She pottied and I noticed her Depends. We walked down the hall to the elevator and she was less wobbly.

We had a long walk to the dining room but she did well. We were seated with tablecloth, napkins, and silverware. The room was bright with high ceilings and Mardi Gras décor. Mom kept commenting on how cheery it was and noticed the people. She put her napkin in her lap right away. We were served good cabbage soup with a side of potato salad. A spoon for each. Mom enjoyed both. We ordered lemon chicken and BBQ ribs. I took some of her plate so as not to overwhelm her. People thought she was almost normal and she enjoyed it and became quite sociable. After lunch, we walked down the hall and she noticed the outdoors.

"Can we go outside?" she asked, bright-eyed.

"Sure."

We walked into the courtyard and down the path to the tables and chairs.

"Let's sit down in the sun," she suggested.

We watched the two big yard cats. They inspected us while we watched them. It was a lovely afternoon and Mom was coming back into the world I had taken her from.

DAD

Thursday, January 24th

Joined Dad for breakfast on our way to Atlanta for our granddaughter Elena's birthday. Dad was showered and shaved and at breakfast. He had a small cut on his cheek and had sat in the hall for a while before or after his shower and gotten cold. He ate well, some coughing—maybe smaller bites? Went to his room to brush teeth and put on Chapstick. Was told by Margaret (medicine dispenser) that Dad had a fall on top of the aide getting out of bed and it took three of them to maneuver him. She mentioned Hoya lift and I said no twice. Rolled him to rehab. He was getting his left arm iced for swelling and then to do some physical therapy. He's tired and a little disoriented.

Saturday, January 26th

Kiki and Michael went to have breakfast with Bapa, and found him in bed still asleep. They got the aide to get him ready for the day and rolled him down to breakfast.

10:30 a.m. Kelly and I went to find Bapa getting his wounds dressed. We alerted the wound nurse about stitches—they were to come out on the twenty-ninth, she knew nothing but would look for orders. He is still bleeding from the hospital IVs. He was in his wheelchair so we rolled him outside for fresh air, sunshine and a talk. I thought we should set some goals again.

"I've got my car right around the corner. Do you want to go for a ride?" I asked.

"Sounds like a deal,." he said.

"The Wingate is just being built. Let's get you out before it's finished. Do you want to stay here?"

"I don't think I can do it, it's so much work. I just want to sleep. I like being lazy."

"OK, but let's try."

3:30 p.m. Denny and Michael visit. He's in his wheelchair facing the wall. He says he called for the nurse to go to the bathroom fifteen minutes ago, but no one showed up to help him and he now needs to be changed. Finally a nurse shows up, cleans him, and leaves him in the bed. Michael and Denny maneuver him into the wheelchair. He has to go potty, so Michael gets the urinal, Denny undoes his diaper. They then go outside to the sunshine. Bapa thinks he can get strong enough to get out of the wheelchair.

"Do you want to go for a ride?"

"No."

"You don't have to drive. I'll take you."

"Not yet."

Sunday, January 27th

7:30 a.m. Michael went and had a hard time waking up Dad; he was very disoriented. Peaches helped get him up and cleaned him. They went to breakfast. He was still foggy and just ate grits. Kelly and I went over at 10 a.m. He was asleep in bed with his mouth wide open. He wanted to be lazy and not wake up. We had Megan and Jennifer (RNs) meet with us about Dad as we were concerned. His legs are swollen and he's lethargic. Michael talked with his nephrologist and he said he would order new blood work if we wanted. So around noon we stopped at the Living Center and ordered it. Michael and I went back at 5 p.m. and Dad was awake and said he thought he was going to die. Especially if he did not get to the toilet, so he pushed the button. Peaches was still on and she arrived. She and Michael helped Dad to the toilet. While not perfect, Dad thought he had achieved a lot, and did stand up at the toilet.

He redressed and we went early to dinner, took the outdoor route, then Michael brought cards to play Mississippi Stud and blackjack. A few residents mentioned how much they liked poker. Turkey, lima beans, and mashed potatoes came, along with milk, pudding, and a cookie. Dad did well—small bites, small sips. Said he didn't know what he'd do without us. A few leg exercises before bed and he brushed teeth, then Peaches came to help finish getting him into his pajamas.

Monday, January 28th

Michael is there at 7:50 a.m. Dad is eating cream of wheat and eggs, toast with jelly, milk, and coffee. Small bites, small sips. His hand is a little less swollen. He pushed himself to physical therapy. They feel his arms and notice an indentation. That's all. Said "we" need to put something under his arm to lie flat.

I join Dad at lunch. He is unshaven, his teeth are unbrushed, and hair is unkempt. The aide told me his tongue was bleeding and the nurse had cleaned it. After eating, he said he thought he was finished (liked the hummingbird cake). I asked if he needed to go to the bathroom, he said no.

"What do you want to do?"

"Go to physical therapy."

First I showed him the outside from the front door. It is warm, but a little cloudy. We then headed back to the room to get Chapstick and brush his hair. Brittany came to do breathing therapy and went to find Dr. Matt. Dad fell asleep in his wheelchair. He wanted to nap, not do physical therapy at this point. We met with Dr. Matt. Dad is lacking in potassium, and this could explain his glazed look. He thought the wraps on his legs and arms would help with the swelling. I ask Dr. Matt if I should keep pushing him to succeed, or back off. He said do it until he gets mad. I said he'd never get mad at me.

"Do you have children, Dr. Matt?"

"Two boys. I get mad at them."

I got Dad into bed for a nap, and headed to the airport to pick up my brother again.

Tuesday, January 29th

It was great to see Dad standing up. Maybe I should get him some parallel bars to stand and walk between. I stood behind the wall and watched him swing his legs side to side and kick the beach ball. He's working hard. The physical therapist said he must have a lot of pain with his arthritis. She can hear and feel it in his shoulders as they pop in and out, and can feel it in his shoulder blades to the middle of his back, but she said he tries very hard to get up. She doesn't know if he can get the strength back to raise himself out of a chair or off a bed or a toilet without help. His creatine level has shot up to 4.5 so we'll try more liquids to flush him. Tammy and Pam came to visit before dinner so he had quite a smile on his face. He really enjoys cutting up with them.

Wednesday, January 30th

His numbers are better, but both heart and kidney doctors are concerned. Dad's legs hurt, wrapped really tightly and elevated. Dinner in bed. Yuk! We stopped by at nine since he had been so miserable. "Life can be good," he says. We straighten him up in the bed—he was cold—readjust the pillow, give him a kiss, and leave. We tell him we're almost out of January.

Thursday, January 31st

I left Mom and headed to see Dad before the meeting with the rehab staff. At the beginning it seemed that having a meeting in two weeks was moot because he would be out by then. Now we're talking months. Alan had joined him for breakfast, still in the room. He ate next to nothing. It was shower day, so he was left in the hall to languish, then late to physical therapy. Not happy. He had pooped his pants at lunch so wanted to just nap. "I'm lazy." Everyone in the staff meeting said he's doing well, working through the arthritis-edema pain. The case manager was going to consult with Dad's heart and kidney doctors to coordinate meds again. We'll meet tomorrow with the dietary to plan tastier meals that Dad might actually eat. There are a hundred people here to fix food for and everyone is a little different.

2 p.m. Went back to the room to find Dad asleep in the wheelchair by the bed.

"Do you want me to wheel you to PT? They didn't come to get you?"

"No, I'm lazy. I want to nap."

I met Briana and Jilly who will be his regulars on the 2 p.m.–10 p.m. shift, so I requested a few things: going to the bathroom in the bathroom, no sleeping past 4:30 p.m., partial dentures out at night as he's biting his tongue bloody. It looks like raw hamburger. I hope they don't burn out, Briana and Jilly. The VA wants to see Dad to evaluate for extra benefits next month, but he can't make it into New Orleans right now. I come away exhausted and dejected and it's only midafternoon. Do I have to go back for dinner?

MOM

Mom was seated in the circle, with unwashed wild hair and a blank look behind her dirty glasses. She smiled as Alan and I crossed the room to sit beside her. It was a few hours after lunch and Fabian was scheduled to play the piano downstairs. We thought it would be a good outing into a different world, rather than the circle. She got up with assistance and wobbled forward. I had her arm which she offered. This docile, dependent woman is not my Mom.

"I don't think we can go," she said.

"It's OK," I said. "There's a concert downstairs and everyone will be going. We'll just be first."

I helped her down the hall to her apartment. She didn't recognize her name on the door. We went in and I sat her at the table with her jigsaw and she started in on it. Alan got a Boost from the refrigerator, an aspirin, and a Claritin.

I demonstrated how to chew the aspirin and her claw-like, unmanicured hands picked up the aspirin and chewed it, then she reached for the Boost. I really have to arrange for a manicure for her, but there's never anyone at the front desk to ask when I am leaving. She's never had fingernails before. She's forgotten that she used to bite them. I clean her glasses, put some Chapstick on her, and try to tame her greasy hair. Tomorrow is Shower Day, and they should wash her hair. It hasn't been washed since she got here.

"It's time to go downstairs," I say.

She questions me with her eyes and I repeat. She struggles to get up from the chair. There's just no strength in those skeletal legs—the long legs of the can-can dancer in the Lions Club plays. Ta ra ra boom tea ay. We walk back to the elevator. She's a little stronger now but her right foot is turning out a little and dragging. This is new. We go downstairs and the chairs are set up in front of the shiny grand piano, but it must still be early so we go out into the courtyard, into the sunshine.

"Look at the big dog."

"That's a cat, Mom."

"Oh, yes," and she points a finger at her head and shoots herself. We watch the big cats and enjoy the sunshine. She has her watch on and she keeps telling us the time. Is it her link to the real world? We get up to go inside. She has found a way to get out of the chair by herself. We walk in

and take a chair. Fabian has not shown up to play the concert, so we will do karaoke. I just hope Mom doesn't make
a commotion as she usually loudly criticizes anyone singing
off-key. She and Dad sang in the choir at St. Mark's when
they were through with the War and a young happy couple
starting a business in Casper. I came across an old news-
paper article while sorting through pictures and memora-
bilia at their house. Mom was coming back to Casper from
Berkeley on Christmas break and was giving a vocal pres-
entation for the public. She was a political science major.
Who knew?

We politely enjoyed the karaoke. Mom just rolled her
eyes when I looked at her. She was behaving, but letting
me know that she was in agreement that it was not good.
Her little coughing started to subside as I have given her a
prescribed cough pill. The ones that no one gives her this
week. Nor her puzzle books. Nor her dignity.

Saturday, February 2nd

Groundhog Day. Got over to Mom's around 2:30 after
Michael, Alan, and I lunched on shrimp po'boys and onion
rings at SouthSide Café. I saw through the door that her
hair had not been done. I walked over to where she was
seated on the couch and noticed her teeth weren't in. She
didn't want to get up. Finally I got her to stand up and

she said she had to go to the bathroom, so I walked her across the room and told the aide she needed to go to the bathroom and she asked did we want to take her to her apartment. I said, "No, she needs to go now. Here she is." I asked the other aide why Mom's hair wasn't washed and where were her teeth? She didn't know, check with Victoria. Michael, Alan, Mom, and I walked down to her apartment after her bathroom and got her teeth brushed and the denture in. She looked in the mirror. "My hair is horrible. Let me try to do something with it."

Michael and I headed down to talk with Victoria. "Do you have five minutes to talk about Mom?"

"Sure, let's go in here," she replied.

We went into the library while I rehearsed in my mind what to say so as to accomplish something and not be rude.

"I really like the routine for Mom you put up on her cupboard door, but I'm not certain it's being followed. Mom's hair hasn't been shampooed since she got here and I think there's only been one shower. I thought she was supposed to be bathed Wednesdays and Saturdays, but that hasn't happened this week. And her teeth aren't in."

"I'll find out what happened, but sometimes she objects so the aides are instructed not to force them to do anything as the resident could get hurt. Their skin is just like paper."

"Is there a chance she could get a shower tomorrow even if it is Sunday? I could come over early to observe and help find out about Mom's behavior. Oh, and she doesn't have a bra on either."

"I personally pulled out her laundry yesterday so I'll find out why and get back to you. I'll let the aide know not to wake her and get her ready for the day until you get here."

Guess I'll set an alarm for 6 a.m.

Sunday, February 3rd

Up at six, at Memory Lane before seven. Lights are on in Mom's apartment. We go in and Katrina says Mom was up at 12:30, 5:00, and a little bit ago. I stick my head into the bedroom and she says hi above the covers.

"Good morning. Let's get in the shower and get ready for the day."

"No," she replies, "not today."

"Mom, yesterday you looked in the mirror and commented on how bad your hair looked, so let's get it washed and get all pretty for the day."

Reluctantly, she gets up. I ask the aide when sheets are changed as I am noticing some marks on the upper sheet.

"Every two days, when laundry is done."

She and I guide Mom to the bathroom, reminding her she's going to take a shower. I tell Katrina I put shampoo on her head before she gets in the shower. That way she remembers to rinse it out. Katrina gets the water on and

Mom into the shower. It's an open stand-up shower with a telephone head. I step away but hear her complaining.

"It's too cold. It's too hot. It's too cold." Finally Mom succumbs and says, "That feels good."

She has always enjoyed being warm. We get the hair dryer out and I explain to Katrina that I had Mom do as much as she could, like drying her own hair, so she wouldn't forget. Then I just finish it up. We put cream on her face, have her brush her teeth and put her dentures in, put on Chapstick. Katrina had started changing the bed, but I had Mom sit on it and put on shoes and socks, then I got her hearing aids. She looked at them as foreign objects. "What am I supposed to do?"

"First you close them like this," I replied and handed her one. "Red is for right. This goes in the right ear." I handed it to her. She had no idea how to get it in. I don't think she's done this for a week or two, and that's how easily she forgets.

2 p.m. It's a beautiful day outside, 70 degrees, so I go to get Mom to bring her home and sit on the patio. I sit down beside her in the circle at Memory Lane and say, "Let's go out in the sunshine." She struggles to get up from the deep couch cushions and we stagger down to her apartment to go potty and get a jacket. I notice she's still in undies, that they haven't put her in Depends. (Yay!) We walk down the hall, go down in the elevator, and leave the building. Mom

is chattering in some strange language, not making sense. If you live with zombies you become one. Riding in the car, she is starting to form sentences, but putting in unorthodox words. She starts reading the billboards and commenting on the street, the city, the contrails above, and she's almost back on this planet. I correct her choice of words and try to have a conversation with her, commenting on what she's saying.

"It seems to me that you had something to do and hadn't done it yet."

"What did I have to do, Mom?"

"Something…I don't really know."

We sit out on the patio and listen to the woodpecker, the traffic noise, the breeze rustling the leaves. We drink a Boost (her) and a beer (me). We have cheese and crackers. She pets Maddie, our dog, who lies beside her. It was like old times, except Dad was missing. The sun started to drop down, it got colder, so we headed inside to work on the jigsaw we had started two weeks ago when she stayed with us. Only two weeks ago.

DAD

Friday, February 1st

Finally, a new month. Hopefully we can put all this behind us. Only one month ago I had two parents not in wheelchairs, not in Depends, living in their own home. Did I see this coming? Maybe eventually like a slow slide into second base, a graduate introduction to assisted living, to not driving, to enjoying the camaraderie and entertainment and transportation in assisted living. We all met with Dietary this morning to plan a menu that Dad would actually eat, rather than shoving a Boost at him. Found out that chopped doesn't really mean chopped but ground up—a perennial dry sausage sitting on his plate. Found out sauces and gravies do exist, just ask. Found out Dad doesn't like summer squashes. I fix steamed zucchini, onions and summer squash all the time for him and Mom. He loves corn but can't have it because of the husk. He loves a bowl of ice cream at night—yes, we can do that. A whole list of food was presented for likes and dislikes and his reaction, with a shrug, was "comme ci, comme ca." But his eyes did light up at ice cream. I think I'll become a gourmet cook at meals, mixing foods on his tray and asking for more ingredients. I'll get creative.

Lunch was shrimp creole—miniscule shrimp taken too early from their mothers, tomato sauce and rice. He ate it all. He was still in his "comme ci, comme ca" mood, though. I asked what he did at PT and he said, "Nothing. I took off my T-shirt and put it back on. I wiped my butt." Alan and I took him outside to show him the sunshine. It was almost 70 degrees. I gave him my sunglasses to wear and we sat in silence, listening to the hammers of the workers next door building the hotel. We took him back to his room and got an aide to take him into the bathroom, to relearn some social skills rather than "just go in my diaper."

Saturday, February 2nd

Michael and Alan spent the morning with Dad, breakfast and some bed exercise, then the gospel sing-along. After lunch he went down for a nap with instructions to Liz to get him up by three. We arrived at 5:30 and he was sound asleep in a dark room. Meghan said she had asked him at three to get up and he said he wanted to sleep. We had a hard time awakening him and he stank. Convinced him that it was dinnertime and he had slept all afternoon. "No muscle is building while you are sleeping," I reminded him. Meghan and Liz got him cleaned up, then he bit his tongue again and it started bleeding. We wheeled him down to the dining room and his tray came right out. However, it had corn (remember that's a no-no right now), no glass for his carton of milk, stringy chicken, and mashed potatoes. I asked for gravy and another vegetable. I got a bowl of gravy and mashed cauliflower. We added butter to it and that was dinner. He didn't eat the gravy/mashed potato/chicken concoction I fixed up, nor the corn on his mashed potatoes that he always had at the casino.

"I feel like life is passing me by," he said nonchalantly.

"What do you mean?" I asked.

"I don't know…"

After dinner, we rolled him around the halls twice, making him use his feet for some of it. We were tired, so we went back to his room and gave him a Boost. Then we rolled him into the bathroom to brush his teeth and clean his dentures. Michael thought he could get him into bed, but Dad was dead weight, not helping at all and his feet slid between Michael's legs. Finally we got him onto the bed and called the aide to rearrange him. I think he was scared as he had quite a look on his face that never went away. Guess we won't try that again. We are so emotionally drained. I'm a little hesitant to leave him tonight after the look on his face and earlier news that the elegant lady with gray braided hair whom we saw at dinner each night passed away. Dad likes to sleep so much, and then worries because he's sleeping so much. Maybe it will just be peaceful.

Sunday, February 3rd

Came to Dad's for breakfast after seeing Mom. He was already at the table with a glazed look. We got him some applesauce for his frosted flakes and a glass for his milk. He liked the frosted flakes-applesauce-milk mélange, it's what he has at home. We wheeled him around the living center, having him do some pulling with his legs, then some neck exercises. Inquired about 9:30 Sittercise and no one knew anything, so Michael and I opened the door to the activities room and searched for the Sittercise video and put it on for Dad. He did pretty well, then got tired so we took him back to the room, called the aide, and left to go have our breakfast and take the car through the car wash. Back at lunchtime to check that he got up to eat, which he did, but then he slept all afternoon. We came back at five after dropping Mom off at her new home. It was Super Bowl Sunday and they did have the game on in the dining room. Dad was seated alone so we joined him. His tablemates came later and were seated with their backs to the TV. Guess they didn't care too much about the game.

Dad's dinner came: chili. It smelled good and I was envious, but Dad just looked at it. I commented on it being a staple Super Bowl fare. He didn't want crackers in it, but took a few bites. Drank his milk, didn't want his cookie, ate his cooked apples. We watched the game. It looked like he was watching it. Then halftime came. We were the only ones left in the dining room and I was enjoying it, then Dad wanted to go to his room, he had pooped his diaper, so I suggested we get an aide to clean him up, then come back and watch the game. Michael came back alone; Dad wanted to go to sleep. So I walked down to his room and said good night, wondering what the night would bring.

Monday, February 4th

7:30 a.m. Michael joined Dad for breakfast (Dad's, not Michael's). I didn't hear from him so felt Dad had made it through the night and I wasn't needed to hurry over. I called Michael to check our phone line which wasn't working well. Must have something to do with the blackout last night in the Superdome! He said it was OK but not going well. Dad was in the dining room when Michael got there, with a pancake, toast, OJ, scrambled eggs, milk, frosted flakes. He ate with both fork and spoon, so a little progress. Then he went back to his room and sat. I came by after eleven and he must have been at PT so I tracked down his case manager to report another bad weekend, what we had said in our meeting that we were trying to avoid. No Sittercise Sunday (except us); cajoling for it on Saturday. Dad's sleeping and depressed.

This morning Dad said, "I'm worried."

Michael asked, "About what?"

Thursday and Friday, February 7th and 8th

We left him alone for a few days—sink or swim—and went to Houston to a five-year-old's birthday party, upbeat spirits, ice skating, putt-putt, and a steak dinner with loved ones. Dad survived on his own. He looked rosy, less edema, fairly clearheaded, a pound less of fluid. He did Sittercise every morning and enjoyed it. I brought Mom over to see him this afternoon and he got teary, whispering, "I love you," "You're so beautiful," and holding hands. I left them alone for a few minutes and thought I was brilliant. They both just wanted to be together.

MOM

Friday, February 8th

I met Mom for lunch. She was seated at the table with a napkin, fork, and spoon. I told her we were going downstairs to have lunch and Michael was joining us. She didn't quite understand that she could leave the other ladies at the table without being rude, as they didn't really care. We went out the door and she was impressed that I knew the codes to get out. We rode the elevator down and started swaying toward the dining room when she announced she needed to go to the bathroom. We turned around and walked toward it, got there, and she said she just went. I asked what she meant "just went," remembering Dad's "just going" in the Depends in front of me. "I just went upstairs." So we turned around and started down one hall, then another toward the private dining room, opened the door, and there was Victoria with a meeting going on. I mentioned there must be a misunderstanding as we were supposed to have the dining room. She just looked at me, so I said we'd leave, and we headed to the main dining room to ask someone if we should sit there. Then I saw Victoria leave down the hall and I wondered if she was checking on it too. The aide in the dining room said it would be fine to sit in there and showed us to the table, as Mom had been hugging the wall, unable to stand free and clear.

We ordered coffee, it came, and I gave Mom a packet of Sweet & Low. She studied it for a while until I demonstrated how to open it. She opened it and stirred it into her coffee. Then she grabbed the sugar container and started reading the packets, then taking them out and sorting them to put them back in. She couldn't find where the creamer packets went so I grabbed them from her and stuck them in the container at the back. "Oh my God!" She scowled and I wondered if everyone was looking at us thinking we belonged upstairs. Michael and the girls showed up to join us for lunch and it went fairly well. She was behaving fairly well, so I thought I could handle her in the car and took her to see Dad.

We walked down the hall at the Living Center to his room and he was having his breathing treatment, looking like someone from Star Wars. He got tears in his eyes when he saw Mom; they held hands briefly and his breathing treatment stopped and he was whisked into the bathroom for a few moments. I put Mom in a straight-back chair as she has been complaining about her back, and Dad sat facing her in the wheelchair. He kept saying he loved her and how beautiful she was and she was quite happy about all that. They chatted away for a while with endearments, then it turned strange—Mom thinking they were getting married and that I, at various moments, was either the minister or her mother. She alluded to the fact that since they were getting married, or just married, they could check into the room, and then she patted the bed. This thrill of marrying Dad went on and on. I couldn't figure out if he was understanding it or not, but he was explaining that they were married and had two children and I was one of them. I thought we should leave and started coaxing her to get up when luckily the wound nurse and two others came in to draw blood from Dad. We walked down the hall, Mom and I, and she chattered that she was getting married. We got back in the car to go to her apartment, and she started talking in a falsetto voice which I later recognized as baby talk. She was back seat driving and very upset that I was on the highway instead of the service road.

"Look at all the cars. Are they here for me?" We got to Memory Lane and I parked the car and went to get her out. "Do I have to go? It's so pleasant here." I don't know if she meant the sunshine or the outside world.

DAD

Sunday, February 10th

I was awakened early by a phone call from Heritage Manor. Dad was being taken to the hospital. He had been helped into the wheelchair to go to the bathroom and then the aide noticed blood seeping through the Ace bandages onto the floor. The wound nurse evaluated his leg and found a long gash on the outside of his right leg. They couldn't stop the bleeding so were sending him to the hospital for stitching. Michael and I met him there. He was asleep in room 5 of the emergency room. Lots of blood. Dr. Mike undid the bloody bandage and there was a leg gash. I thought back to the days of the meat locker at Grant Street Grocery and the sides of meat hanging from the hooks and saw how much Dad's leg resembled that.

Three inner stitches and fifteen outer stitches later and we were ready to go back to Dad's home away from home—Heritage Manor. But the bus wasn't running. We were asked how comfortable we felt transporting him there ourselves (essentially one block) and we replied, "Not at all." We can't maneuver him. He becomes dead weight and we don't know the techniques, so an ambulance was ordered. An hour later Dad was awakened from a dead sleep to be lifted from the hospital bed to the ambulance stretcher. His eyes looked at me, terrified, and he asked, "Where are we going, Lib?" I told him we were going back to Heritage Manor, to his rehab room, and tried to reassure him. When we got back to Heritage Manor and he was rolled down the hall, he still had the look of terror on his face, and was asking me where he was going. The ambulance attendants aligned him beside his bed and lifted him, sheets and all, onto the bed. Peaches came to get him cleaned up and we left him to sleep the afternoon away and recover from all the lifting. Michael went back at dinnertime to check on him and he was having dinner in bed.

Tuesday, February 12th

Dad was disoriented at breakfast, rehab, and lunch. He slept in the afternoon in his wheelchair in the room. When Kelly and I got there, Pam and Tammy were sitting on his bed visiting with Dad. He was in the wheelchair facing them, drinking from a green cup. Pam had brought him a small martini with lots of olives. His eyes were rolling, looking up at the ceiling, side to side, never focusing on anyone. I'm not sure he recognized me. He certainly didn't know Kelly. I was glad to see Tammy and Pam as they always bring a smile to Dad, but he was pretty disoriented. I took the green cup away and we visited some. Dad thought he had been betting a lot of money at the casino last night. Larry, his roommate, said he might have gone to Bingo at the rehab center. Dad kept thinking he was holding the cup but he was just holding his new claw-like left hand and wrist. He didn't want to drop the cup, which he didn't have. He thought he had missed his appointment with Dr. Roberts, a doctor he had a long time ago. I thought it best we get some dinner in him. Michael had now replaced Kelly, and Pam and Tammy had left, after some lewd sexual comments. I think if Dad had had his wits around him he could have participated in the repartee, but he was pretty far lost. He couldn't figure out how to lift his feet up so we could push his wheelchair to the dining room. I asked Peaches to help us and she recommended pulling him backward, which we did. We put lots of liquids in him at dinner in case of dehydration—two glasses of water, a carton of milk, and coffee. Dinner was a shredded meat burger which I doctored with a slice of cheese, tomato, pickle, lettuce, onion, and some gravy. No to the tater tots, but yes to the ice cream. He imitated his tablemate a lot, reaching for things not there, and very shaky. His sentences were good but wrong. I did not "cycle" over yesterday nor was I in PT waiting for a cycle. I was not at the casino with him last night waiting for a slot machine. We took him back to the room. He couldn't get his dentures out, so Michael donned some gloves and helped him. Peaches came to get him cleaned up and into bed. I asked her to look after him well as he wasn't himself.

MOM

Tuesday, February 12th

I hadn't visited Mom for a few days as I was so preoccupied with Dad. I found her getting ready for lunch in "the room" but without glasses. The aides didn't know what had happened as they had looked but couldn't find them. She had had a shower that morning in the main shower as she was dressed early and didn't want a shower. I bet that was fun! I asked Kelly to go to Mom's room and check her purse for the glasses, as Mom can't see without them. She found them under the bed, along with a pair of black shoes. I noticed Mom's lips were still quite chapped, so an aide appeared with Mom's Chapstick. Mom was quite glad to see us. I had brought her bridge magazine so we talked about bridge and I reminded her when she and I went to tournaments and got some trophies. I told her Kelly wanted to learn to play bridge and that Mom had taught bridge lessons for years.

I talked Precision and Michaels and we agreed to meet on Thursday for bridge lessons.

Kelly and I then headed over to Mom and Dad's house to catalog and photograph to start selling some of the art stuff—Oriental and European. I started grouping birds, vases, lamps, and just remembering the stories behind their belongings. I think every place in the world was visited by them over the years.

I grabbed Mom's hairdryer and a stuffed dog that sang "Singing in the Rain" to take back to her. It was still raining when we pulled into Memory Lane. Mom was seated with her hearing aids out because of the sing-along. I convinced her to get up and come with me down to her room. We put the hearing aids back in and showed her the dog. She picked up the dog and started cuddling and rocking it. I had a very hard time getting her to give up the dog so that I could put it on the chair and turn it on to start singing and dancing. She started singing along and moving her arms like a showman, just like she had done many times before. I put Chapstick on Mom, combed her hair, and got her out of the chair to go back to the dining room. It's not very far down the hall, but she certainly gets out of breath and starts wheezing at any exertion.

DAD

Wednesday, February 13th (Ash Wednesday)

He was better but still not himself. I saw Andrew, the director of Dad's facility, and mentioned the fiasco last night when I inquired about Dad's meds—what he was now getting, and was he really getting them. Something to explain the new weird behavior. He tested Dad and ruled out a stroke. Three nurses visited and we consulted, trying to figure out Dad's depths and find out what was going wrong, why he was deteriorating so. Then we left to drive back to Houston with Kelly and the girls for Valentine's Day. On the road, I received a call from Patrick, head of nursing, that he had inspected Dad's legs and heels after I had complained that his wraps on the arms and legs were not coming off at night to give him some air. He said Dad had cellulitis, an infection in his wounds and heels, and needed to go to a facility for long-term acute cure with IV antibiotics, so now we get to evaluate that. Maybe we can get him back into the hospital for IV and his regular heart and kidney doctors who have known him for years. But then what?

Thursday, February 14th

Dad is sent over to the hospital emergency room and evaluated by the hospital doctor, who saw him for the eight days in January. He asked when I last saw him, which was just a day ago. Dad is dehydrated, his legs look like hamburger and are infected, and he's pretty incoherent. He is put on IV for saline and antibiotics.

E-mail from Mike and Libby Bentson

Dear Loved Ones,

Dad went back into the hospital last night and is doing much better with an IV of fluids and antibiotics but it is not long term. We have decided to become aggressive about this and give him a good quality of life for a brief time so tonight he is receiving a transfusion and tomorrow will have a port inserted for dialysis as all the fluids he is receiving plus the fluid in his lungs and around the heart will cause the kidneys to fail so need to be ready for dialysis. When stable, he will come to my house and we will set up the den for him. Two doctors have talked to me today about hospice, so I will see what the week brings and make necessary arrangements. Jennifer, Denny, Alan, and their families have all been with us helping so much, and we thank everyone for all their prayers. Cal, when we get Dad settled, we welcome you and Jo to come visit us.

Mom is settled at the Memory Center. It is hard to crush an independent spirit to conform to the rules of the group so each day is a new issue, but she is safe there.

MOM

Thursday, February 14th (Valentine's Day)

I had planned to go see Mom and take her a rose in a vase, but with Dad's extreme downturn I didn't have the strength. Michael had given me a singing card—Rascal Flatts—and a kalanchoe, then we drove back from Houston.

Friday, February 15th

Victoria greets me with, "What anxiety med is Mom on? She needs some."

> "What the hell, Marian?" Dad had just gotten home from a long day at the store to find Mom seated in their living room, a sledgehammer at her feet, an Old Fashioned in her hand, and a smile on her face. Dinner was on the stove, and Alan and I were playing with plastic bricks.

"Oh, I thought we needed a bigger bedroom, so I knocked out the wall." And together that summer, they reconfigured the house on Boxelder. Dad's brother Cal came from Pittsburgh to work at the store for the summer, help move walls at the Boxelder house, and when that was finished, they built the garage.

Then Mom decided we needed a bomb shelter. Alan and I thought that would be pretty cool, like a fort or something. Every weekend and in the evenings, we went to Grant Street Grocery, down the stairs to the basement, across the cement floor between the cases and cases of toilet paper, paper towels, and paper products where we had made a path, to the far corner room and we started clearing it out and cleaning it. The walls were cement, all the way up to the ceiling, which was the floor of the store itself, with massive beams as our ceiling. Mom hung curtains all around to make it homey. We set up cots and sleeping bags, and moved in canned goods for supplies. We tested the massive door to make sure it would close tightly. This was fun! We brought in candles and matches, some of my favorite dolls, some of Alan's favorite toys, including Pippo the clown. We would now be safe for the Cold War.

Elmer, Charlie, Lou, and Walt, every Tuesday night they got together to play bridge, or poker, or gin rummy. Each took a turn hosting at his house with plenty of nuts, candy, and desserts made by their tolerant, loving spouses. In between hands, they discussed the topics of the day, the topics of the town:

> "I see Mullens' got a new car on his lot. A Cadillac. Black with long fins and nice whitewalls. He called to see if I might be interested. Think I might go drive it."

> "Gordon called. They're putting together a deal on a gas well west of town. Wanted to know if I was interested in getting in on the deal."

> "There's quite a ruckus going on in Cuba. Our reserve unit might be called up. Guess Marian can run the store for a while." (Dad had stayed in the reserves after WWII and was in the Casper Air Force Reserve squadron, and was still eligible for combat duty.)

Casper College advertised senior classes for residents over fifty-five, so Mom and Dad signed up for xeriscape, architecture, accounting, and finance. Grant Street Grocery was flourishing, maybe because of the business acumen Dad was developing from his classes and maybe because of his pleasing personality. He would open the store at eight every morning except Sunday, put on a pot of coffee, and greet the Bunny Bread delivery man. Then he would grab a donut, fix a cup of coffee, and visit with his early shoppers and his loyal staff, finding out what pleased people, what he needed to stock at the store, and how he could help in the community. I think there was a little political talk, but Mom talked Dad out of running for city council or buying into a Casper bank board. She was just content with their pleasant life and didn't want to rock the boat. From her accounting class at the college, she went on to learn about investing and started to do some stock market trading, complete with options, puts, and calls. She had an index card box where she recorded all her transactions, profits and losses, and started to do quite well. Her stock market profits went into her travel account, and she presented Dad, as well as Alan and me, and later our families, with some fantastic travel opportunities. Her analytical mind was also at work analyzing the new game of duplicate bridge. The drinking and partying days of Viva La Joie were becoming bridge games and tournaments—regionals and nationals—then teaching bridge and conversations, rehashing bridge hands and strategies. She and Dad became the first and third Life Masters in Wyoming and continued playing bridge long after dementia set in; and Mom couldn't remember if she had lunch, but could still win at bridge!

DUPLICATE CONTRACT CLUB prize winners, who brought home trophies from a tournament in the Black Hills recently. Seated are Mrs. Neal Walker and Mrs. W. E. Schlessman, and standing are R. C. Williams, Neal Walker, W. E. Schlessman and Dr. Bryce _____ the trophies they brought home—(Tribune-Herald Photo)

Newly Promoted Reservists

Four members of the 9757th Air Reserve Squadron of Casper were recently promoted. The officers and the new rank are (left to right) Major A. E. Deru, commanding officer Lt. Col. Roy Hill, Major W. E. Schlessman, and Major James M. Wolfe.—STAR photo.

Remembering his South Pacific route in WWII
at the WWII Museum in New Orleans

MOM

Saturday, February 16th

Mom throws a glass of water on a resident.

Sunday, February 17th

She's covered in a black blanket and refuses to leave the circle. Jennifer, our daughter, and her two children, Zach, and Elena say hi.

Monday, February 18th

The Memory Center called. Mom has an infection on her shin where she had stitches. I go to check, but she refuses to leave the circle. Michael invites her for cocktails; she is loud and obnoxious. I try to turn her hearing aids up so she won't be so loud; she complains. She sinks down into the couch. Michael fixes her some cranberry juice, which she slurps. She then burps. She has to go to the bathroom. She grunts and announces, "Here it comes." We walk back to the circle and pass a tall inmate. "She's mean," Mom says.

Tuesday, February 19th

Mom is looking pretty scruffy, so I ask when she might get a shower. The aide says Mom had refused and put up quite a fuss so I make arrangements to come over for 7:30 a.m. tomorrow and help get her in the shower. She had been kind of cleaned up as she had gone to the bathroom in the bathroom sink early that morning. I walk her down the hall and she asks how Dad is. "He's nice, but he's not able to take care of me now. I'll have to find someone else."

Wednesday, February 20th

Michael and I get up at 6:30 a.m. and head over to Memory Lane. We find Mom in bed asleep, so we sit at the table and wait for the aide. When she comes we go in to wake Mom and find her fully dressed beneath the covers with beads on! And her teeth are on the pillow with her. I cajole her into getting undressed and into the shower as her son is coming into town today. She is loud and complains vehemently about the water—not warm enough, too warm, ah, ah, ah! We get her dressed, teeth in, face creamed, hearing aids in, shoes on, hair blown dry, glasses on, watch on. Then we sit at the table and have some cranberry juice and vitamins before we take her to the dining room for breakfast.

Thursday, February 21st

I got her a doctor's appointment in Diamondhead with her old/new doctor about her leg. Mom is at lunch in the dining room when Alan and I go to get her. A full plate is in front of her, but she is not eating. She motions to Alan to have a chair and tries to order something for him. We tell her we've already eaten, but she is insistent that Alan eat and keeps putting her plate in front of him. I try to take it away to get her up to come with us and she gets loudly mad. We go back and forth with the plate and she calls me rude. Maybe I am, but I'm just trying to get her to the doctor. Finally, we get her to stand up, get her bearings, and start walking down to her apartment to get a coat. The drive is crazy; she is in the back seat chattering away, reading signs but now she doesn't know words.

"MILL ION AIRE. MILLI ON AIRE. DIA MOND HEAD. HEAD! LOOK AT ALL THE CARS!"

We get to the doctor's office but are early so we stop to see Tammy. Tammy gives us a big hug and fixes Mom's hearing aids. There might be some recognition there, I can't tell. We get out of the car to walk to the doctor's office.

"Oh my God! How far? It's cold. Oh my God!"

When inside we sit down and Mom starts sorting through the pamphlets, taking one of each, like a three-year-old. We get her on the scale and she's lost eleven pounds in a month. Ivy comes to take her temperature, oxygen level, and blood pressure. She puts the cuff on Mom and I try to explain to Mom that it will pump up and squeeze her arm for a second. Ivy starts to pump it up but Mom cringes down in the chairs, crying in pain, "Oh please, no, I can't take it, oh please," and then she's quiet. We all think she's playing a game, as usual, then realize she's passed out and think she's dead. She then wakes up. I don't know what her blood pressure was. The doctor comes in and Mom is babbling. I take down her nylons so the doctor can see the infection and Mom cringes, says how mean I am. The doctor addresses Mom, engaging in small conversation. She thinks Mom's rapid decline might be a urinary tract infection, so wants a urine and blood sample and says she'll assist Mom as senses this could become impossible. Mom slinks down the hall dragging her leg as she has started to do, with the doctor assisting her. Alan and I stay out of sight. Ivy tries to draw blood and we hear Mom screaming, pleading, "Oh no, oh no!" The doctor prescribes a strong antibiotic for Mom's leg infection and also for her cough, and sends us for an x-ray to see why Mom is coughing. I drop Alan and Mom off for x-ray and go to

Mom's house to pick up mail and some groceries. When I get back to x-ray, we can't get Mom to stand up as she is busy buttoning her coat, again and again. Another couple in the waiting room helps Mom with the last button and holds the door for us. The ride home is very long.

"You hit something! What did you hit?"

"I didn't hit anything, Mom, that's just the sounds of the highway."

"Look at all the cars. Oh my god!"

Friday, February 22nd

I draw the short straw and get over to Mom's between breakfast and lunch to change the bandage on her leg and give her another antibiotic. All her tests show no UTI; healthy except a bit of pneumonia which we'll treat with the existing antibiotics. Mom tells me she hates me.

Saturday, February 23rd

Alan and I both go over and I get Mom out of the dining room. She is sitting alone at a table not eating but sleeping in the chair. I take her back to her apartment, put a bra and sweater on her, put her teeth in, and give her a Boost. We work on the puzzle, almost finished. She's wet on the pajamas in the dresser drawer.

Sunday, February 24th

I go to see Mom after I go to church to give her the antibiotic and dress her shin. She was seated in the dining room in a lounge chair by herself, snoozing without her glasses. Everyone else was eating. Her hair was wild; no shower. And only one hearing aid. I awakened her; she said she was hungry when I mentioned lunch, so she struggled up and I took her over to a table. The aide brought chicken and broccoli soup so while she started to eat that like a hummingbird, I went to get her medicine and a vitamin. Her hearing aid was in two pieces on her nightstand, so I put that in my pocket to see about getting it fixed. I took her pills back to her, got some cranberry juice, and she got the two big pills down, struggling to swallow with just a sip of juice. The bandage was already off her leg—the childproof, waterproof bandage—so I put ointment and another big bandage on. Carrot and raisin salad came, then a plate of lasagna and a side of summer squash. Too many choices for her. I can see why she isn't eating, she's overwhelmed. I got her to take a few bites, then leave to check on Dad, who was talking about getting up a golf game when I saw him before church. And walking. And standing.

New Year's Day was always great. We would bundle up and head down to Grant Street Grocery to take inventory. January 1 in Casper is always below freezing and the store had cement floors. Alan and I would count the items on the pharmacy shelf: shampoos, toothpaste, bar soap. It wasn't complicated. Then we'd move to the canned vegetables. Mom and Dad would count the high shelves and the cleaning supplies, the produce, and the frozen food. Dad had already done the meat and the penny candy. Alan and I would get finished counting and then play grocery store, getting a basket and going around putting items into our baskets. Then we'd trade baskets and re-stock each other's selections. If Mom and Dad still weren't ready to go, we'd head to the magazine rack and sort through the comic books—*Archie, Superman, Donald Duck*. Our New Year's dinner was at the Hills or the Fullers. Everyone had kids around the same age, so we'd eat and play games or listen to music while the parents ate, smoked, drank, and enjoyed each other's company and stories.

Dad came down with rheumatic fever when Alan and I were young (ten and eight), and went to the hospital. We couldn't visit, so we stood out in the park across the street and he would come to his window and wave down at us. When he finally came home he was not supposed to get out of bed so he read a lot, and we joined him in his room with our armloads of books. I think that was when his brother decided to send him a subscription to *Playboy* magazine too, to keep his spirits up. Finally he could go back to work with strict instructions to take a nap every day. So he set up a cot down in the basement of the Grant Street Grocery and every day after his lunch of a slab of bologna on two pieces of bread, he headed downstairs to take his nap.

After the rheumatic fever came monkey shoes. Dad started developing spurs in his heels from extra calcium deposits and standing on the cement floors of the Grant Street Grocery, only partially covered with sawdust. Mom found a catalog with special shoes to help his feet so she sent away for these black side-tie shoes that resembled monkey feet, before Birkenstocks were invented. He would dress every day in his white short-sleeve shirt that Mom ironed, a tie, and dark pants. And monkey shoes. When he got to the store at 8 a.m., he donned a white butcher's apron, and that was his uniform for almost forty years. And Mom would bleach his butchered-blood aprons and shirts and wash and iron his self-imposed uniform. She had a gas dryer and the pilot light was always going out so she would get a soda straw and light it, get down on her stomach to light the pilot, turn on the gas, push in the straw, and, voila, the pilot light was relit and she could finish the laundry.

DAD

Saturday, February 16th

Our daughter, Jennifer, and her kids arrive and meet me at the hospital at 3:30 when I go to sign consent forms. Dad is doing well after all his drips. The vascular surgeon is coming in to insert the IV lines for dialysis. It is done in the room with lidocaine and now Dad looks like Frankenstein with two tubes coming out of his neck. I warn J and the kids and they still want to see him as they have talked about this and are prepared. Dad is quite congenial and happy to see J and the kids, really moved. The kids are great, very loving toward him. Zach is quite moved, but stoic, and Elena very talkative. Dad will go into dialysis this evening and we'll check back on him after dinner at Assunta's. It was a good but long dinner. We saw everyone we knew there, so lots of conversations. Elena falls asleep in the car, so she and I remain in the car while J, Zach, and Michael go to see Dad.

Sunday, February 17th

Dad's doing well. A good choice, I feel, to get the dialysis done. Two liters of fluid off. Dad has great color and we all have a good visit. Dad is feeding himself and eating well. His legs really look good. They are healing, but the stitches from last Sunday are taken out as they weren't holding. At least we got a week in. We all come back after dinner (Sal and Judy's) and things aren't going as well. His numbers might look good but his mind is spacey. He makes a little sense, but he thinks there is a dog in the room or "the man is climbing the curtains."

Monday, February 18th

The hands are really interesting. Dad has just finished his second round of dialysis, one liter off, but he's pretty spacey.

"You're going to kill me yet!" he says when I enter the room.

"Is that what you want?" I ask.

There is no reply. He is now back in his room lying in bed, eyes wide open. His hands, gnarled and curled, keep moving, picking at each other. Sometimes he reaches out and then retracts his arm.

"There are body parts in this hand. Don't drop them," he says. His eyes close but his hands don't stop—shaking, reaching, picking at each other. "I'll pay now, but just for one," he says, then smiles.

It's been a long day and he hasn't been as sharp as usual. Jennifer, Elena, and Zach come to say good-bye on their way back home. Bapa says to Elena how beautiful she is. He remarks on how tall Zach is getting. He smiles at Jennifer and tears well up in his eyes when she kisses him good-bye. She'll be back in a few weeks, but not the kids. On our way down to the elevator, they wonder if this might be the last time they see him. I wonder too.

I see all three of his doctors before noon. His heart doctor comes in and says he looks so much better than when he saw him Friday. He says the heart is doing well. He should know as he's repaired it so many times over the years. Two different bypasses, a valve, and a pacemaker. I think he's grown quite attached to my father. My father calls him a good friend. His hospital doctor comes in and comments on how well the leg wounds are clearing up and mentions four to five more days of IV antibiotics, then oral. He says since he now knows Dad is coming back to my house to stay, he will have a social worker get in touch to let me know what I will need. They will also assign home health and a physical therapist, but we don't have to make plans for four to five days or more. Then the kidney doctor appears and says we'll do another dialysis today and check kidney functions tomorrow, then decide about further dialysis. The port that was put in is a temporary one for this week's dialysis. I call my brother and repeat all this. We'll take each day at a time.

Tuesday, February 19th

All his tests are great, but we can't wake him, nor can the doctor.

Wednesday, February 20th

He's awake this morning, eating a little. And a little spacey.

"I can't remember how this all happened," he says.

"You got the flu."

"I thought I was coming to meet the president."

"What president?"

"You know, of the company. He was giving bonus checks but mine was just $8."

I go to pick Alan up at the airport.

Thursday, February 21st

A good day. The three doctors are amazed after seeing him Tuesday. We have a good visit, but he's not eating much, full after five bites. His hands are unclenched and he's using his left hand, finally.

Friday, February 22nd

Waiting all day for dialysis. He eats about seven bites at each meal. Arms and hands are swelling. PT came and got him to sit at the edge of the bed, but he couldn't stand nor grasp his walker.

"I can't believe how much strength I've lost in four days."

"Try forty days, Dad," I say.

He has rosy cheeks from just that little bit of exercise. We meet with the case manager and set up home health, check into home dialysis, and meet with Skipper to put an addition onto the house—a bath and a bedroom downstairs.

Saturday, February 23rd

Dad said good-bye tonight and asked us to leave—Michael, Alan and I. He said he'd had a great life and thanked us all.

"She'll take it hard," he said and nodded toward the pillow where he thought Mom lay.

"I'll see you in the morning," I said.

"Well, thanks for everything in case I die," he said. "I can't believe it's come to this. I thought I'd die differently."

"How did you think you'd die differently, Dad?"

"I don't know, just not like this."

Alan and I had explained to him he was going to dialysis again, but he looked like a deer caught in the headlights when he and his bed were rolled into the hall to go upstairs to dialysis.

Now Alan and Michael and I sit at the kitchen table and decide no more dialysis. To what end would we want him to disorient so much for one good day when he realizes he can't be who he was last month, or last year. He doesn't have the strength. He said, "It's always something more," and shrugged his shoulders. Always with a smile. I think he's told us he wants no more. So we will bring him to my house where we have set up the bed in the playroom. He'll be at home, with familiar surroundings. His birthday is next Saturday—ninety-four.

MOM

Monday, February 25th

After our vigil with Dad, Michael volunteers to go see Mom and give her antibiotics and dress her shin. I had gotten a call earlier from the director of Memory Lane that I needed to have a meeting. Mom was very disruptive and abusive to several visitors and their loved ones. I said she'd lost eleven pounds since coming there and had a personality change which was behavioral, not clinical, so, yes, I wanted a meeting. Michael found Mom seated at a table by herself by the kitchen, behaving nicely. I wonder what they gave her! Michael brought her the antibiotic and a vitamin and a cookie, then changed the bandage and visited a little. She was charming. She was special.

DAD

Monday, February 25th

We spent yesterday preparing for Dad's homecoming—calling sitter agencies, figuring how long each day we would need people, wondering if Dad had Wednesday and Thursday as good days, then he would start needing dialysis by his birthday Saturday, and if that would be a good day as the family will all be here. I was going to make his favorite cake—angel food. Things started taking a turn for the worse last night around dinnertime at the hospital. "Hold me. Hold me," he kept asking. He was very agitated and thrashing his legs and twitching his arms. We decided to take turns throughout the night and stay with him. Alan drew the middle of the night shift when Dad's temperature rose to 103 degrees. The nurses packed him in ice blankets and by 6 a.m. when I arrived, Dad was less agitated but still mumbling.

"I was the troublemaker, I'm sorry," he said. I said that's OK. "No, I'm not talking to you, I'm talking to your mother!"

"Oh."

He kept asking me to help him sit up so I kept read-justing the bed. I tried aromatherapy and massage to calm him. The good news is he thinks that he can still sit up, that he can stand up, that he can walk. The good news is that he doesn't know how debilitated he has become in fifty days.

Today we met with hospice, to change from home health to hospice at the house. Then we met with one of Dad's doctors, then another, and they felt in-hospital hospice would be what we need as he would only be with us a few hours more. We have to call everyone who was coming into town to spend a good day and share a good-bye. We have to call a funeral home. We have to enjoy every moment before Dad leaves us. I can't imagine what it will be like without my father here. He's always been here.

Tuesday, February 26th

It's amazing; Dad is doing great, awake and fairly lucid, so we've decided to take him to my home where everything is set up for him. The nephrologist comes in, he and Dad talk, tell some jokes, and he takes Dad's ports out of the neck, and says to me that it's been a pleasure, knowing us all, although I am his worst enemy! "Oh no, not you," he always says when he sees me.

Alan will ride with Dad in the ambulance so he's not afraid, so I hurry home to make up the bed. Dad is delivered and swung onto the bed from the ambulance gurney. He has a smile on his face. We place the Valentine lovey that the girls made onto his shoulder and take his smiley photo, texting everyone and saying he's home. He's holding court here in the playroom. Our dog is very happy he's here and there is so much going on now. Hospice comes to introduce themselves and explain things. Oxygen is delivered along with a nebulizer and suction device and a short introduction course on using everything. What am I getting into? A client and friend of mine who's a home health nurse comes over to meet Dad as she'll be here two to three times per day to change his pants and roll him. We'll do the top part, we won't do the bottom part. Dad gets a bed bath, shave, teeth brushed, clothes changed from hospital robe to T-shirt. He's smiling. I elect to spend the night sleeping on the couch in the playroom, just in case. He starts coughing around 4 a.m. and I feel guilty I didn't get the distilled water yet to run the oxygen.

Wednesday, February 27th

Our son and daughter-in-law are on their way in from Houston. They were going to wait until Friday, but Dad might not be doing well by then and they want to have a good visit with him. It's a good day. We're all settling in. You can't wipe the smile off Dad's face. I hook his "loud" phone up near his bed, so he can call a friend or two that has inquired about him. Denny elects to sleep on the couch by his Bapa. We share stories and tears while he sleeps.

Thursday, February 28th

Another great day. The house is full of energy. I told Dad I had brought Mom over to the house yesterday but they were never in the same room. He says he would like to see her, so I bring her over today in the afternoon for a few hours. She stands by his bedside and he tears up telling her how much he loves her, then trying to explain to her why he's lying down in bed. He later says to me how good it was to see Mom, but how much she's deteriorated. He eats great, has a little port wine, and the kids pull up music on their iPhones: Mack the Knife, Tennessee Waltz, Frank Sinatra, Glenn Miller. We put the oxygen on him and he falls asleep. We retire to the kitchen to drink and play cards, a new game called Beanie. I sleep on the couch until six, then get up to go to the bathroom. Dad says hello.

MOM

Wednesday, February 27th

A really bizarre day. Alan and I go to get Mom and bring her back to the house. She walks in right past Dad, into the kitchen, and starts on her Word Finder, which she had been unable to do recently. She is finding words within words, making her own word puzzle. After an hour or two, during which all is pleasant and she has had a Boost and worked on her Word Finder, she slides down in the chair, takes out her teeth and hearing aids, takes off her glasses, closes her eyes, and says she's dying. She closes her eyes and moans. Her hand is missing. Her leg is being pulled off. We don't know if this is a game she is playing so she won't have to leave, or what is going on.

"I'm dying, I'm dying, I have to go to the hospital."

"No, Mom, you have to go to your apartment."

We leave her alone for a few minutes to see if she will calm down. Finally, after about fifteen minutes, we are able to convince her to stand up and go "home" with Alan. She is still insisting she is dying and needs to go to the hospital. We get her teeth back in, her glasses on, her hearing aids in. She minces out to the car and slinks into the back seat. All the way back to Memory Lane, she insists she's dying, then she starts to quit moaning, opens her eyes, and begins to recover. We take her upstairs and it is dinnertime, so we seat her at a table by herself and sit down with her. Almost everyone has finished except for Josie and another woman seated at a table within Mom's line of vision. They are quarreling periodically and sweet Josie has transformed into a nasty crone mumbling "shut up, shut up." I move myself to block Mom's view so that she will concentrate on eating. She keeps offering me some of her soup, but I say I have already eaten and am just ordering a beer. We sneak out when she's almost finished dinner.

Thursday, February 28th

Mom comes over after her lunch. She brings her puzzle book again and pretty much concentrates on it. I think Denny and Kelly should learn to play bridge, so we get out a deck of cards and start explaining. Mom was a great bridge instructor and a Duplicate Life Master. She is quite keen on instructing Alan, Denny, and Kelly and we play a few hands. It gets late and is dinnertime at Memory

Lane, so we take her back. She really didn't want to leave as she really loves the bridge game. We get her settled in for dinner.

DAD

Friday, March 1st

We've made it through January and February. Time flies. Dad is having a good day; a piece of toast with jelly for breakfast, Boost for lunch. Hospice comes to bathe him and order supplies and shave him, rewrap his arms which are weeping, and he's developed a rash under his left arm. After they leave, he feels he needs to go to the bathroom. He uses the urinal quite well. The kidneys seem to be working again.

MOM

Friday, March 1st

Do we see Mom? Do we bring her over? There's so much going on we don't remember. We just react.

Saturday, March 2nd

It's Dad's birthday. We get a call from Memory Lane that they can't control Mom and we need to take her away. We go get her; she eats a good lunch, and enjoys the car ride.

"Look at the cars!" She reads all the billboards to us. Her sentences don't quite come together, some of the words are wrong, but she chatters and chatters. We bring her to the house—it is full of family. She recognizes Dad's brother and family and they all hug. She and Dad hold hands and have a repartee.

"What's wrong?"

"I had the flu."

"Oh, I don't want it!"

"I don't have it anymore."

"Why are you like that?"

"It sent me to the hospital."

Mom comes to the other room where we are all sitting and Kelly gets a magazine to distract her. They read through it, the ads, the recipes. Mom comments on the hairdos, the makeup. The lipstick ad says it makes you more kissable. "The only kiss I'd give her is good-bye!" she says sarcastically.

Around 5 p.m., she starts getting tired and the consensus is she should go back to Memory Lane. I'm afraid she will have missed dinner, but Alan agrees to take her. As they are backing out of the driveway, I grab a coat and run out to go with them. Mom is mumbling about bidding and point count and going to the bridge game. Alan and I say over and over again that there is no game tonight. She gets more agitated. Dinner is over and they've sent the food downstairs, so no dinner for Mom. We take her to her apartment and give her a Boost. She is roaming the apartment going on and on about "two clubs. If you bid it then that means…" She gets more and more aggressive. "Are you here for the game?" We insist there is no game tonight.

"What day is it?"

"Saturday"

"Then that's a good day for a bridge game."

"No, nobody showed up. Let's go to bed."

We take her down to the coven of Memory Lane and try to get her to settle down. I stay behind and watch through the glass door. She and Alan are having a conversation, but he finally gets her settled into a lounge chair. After he leaves, she pops out and starts to walk around the room, confronting residents about whether they're here for the game. She gets right in their face, so I enter and converse with her and lead her out. This is not working. After an hour or so of her insistence on a bridge game and reciting the rules of bridge, we decide on a sleeping pill for her. This is not how we want to spend Dad's birthday dinner celebration. I am cross and won't even take calls from my husband. Alan heads to the drug store to get some sleeping pills. We give her one and dump out a jigsaw puzzle to distract her from the fanaticism of a bridge game. She insists that we not turn the pieces over, but keep the pink undersides visible. She's dealing bridge hands and distributing into four piles. She is mumbling more slowly now, and I am able to approach her, have her hand me her hearing aids, take out her teeth, and then I lead her to the bathroom to brush her teeth and get ready for bed. As she gets into her pajamas, I notice two other scabs on her, one on her back and one on her arm, so I put ointment on them as well as on her leg and hope she doesn't pick at them. As she lies down, she's still talking bridge rules, so Alan and I stay around the corner until she stops mumbling and then we feel it's safe to leave, and we head back to Dad's birthday dinner. It's 8:30 p.m.

DAD

Saturday, March 2nd

Happy Birthday, Daddy. You're ninety-four today. He looks great. The loud phone by his bed rings all day long—dear friends Linda and Shirley, grandchildren, great grandchildren, Terri. His brother and family arrived yesterday and it is great. His niece feeds him and rearranges pillows. We talk about family—his Dad, the family tree, where in Germany did we come from, and what skeletons do we have in the closet! I'm fixing ham for dinner as his brother used to call him "Hamfat" when they were growing up. His brother was "Porky." Kelly frosts the angel food cake in green for St. Patrick's Day and we put clown leprechauns on top. White camellia blossoms and red azalea flowers, all from his yard, are in a bowl by his bed. He stays awake all day and even has wine with dinner. I get called away at lunchtime to pick up Mom as she is causing a ruckus at Memory Lane. Kelly,

Alan, and I have lunch with her and bring her home, which we had planned to do anyway. She and Dad hold hands and chatter to each other, neither one quite hearing the other, but terms of endearment are there. Happy Birthday, Daddy. Two pieces of cake!

Sunday, March 3rd

All that food and drink has made a mess, so the aide is busy. Dad has a good bath, not too much to eat as we choke him on his pills and applesauce and it's a scary moment. He has a Boost and is happy. Denny and Kelly pack up and say good-bye. It's been a good visit and a fun time, so I think they are comfortable leaving and getting back to their little family, although there are tears shed out in the driveway, but what's new. His brother Cal and Jo and their daughter Jodie come over for a couple of hours before they hit the road. Jo says Dad has good color and looks good. I agree. We all have a light conversation and talk again about some family stories. I've gotten out an old photo album as well as the story of Dad's life book, which Jennifer had made for his ninetieth birthday. It's another good day, but after Cal leaves, we begin to see some shaking and confusion. It's like Dad put on a good show while everyone was here, and now we head into reality.

Monday, March 4th

"Oh Lord, please make things better." I come downstairs and Dad is talking in his sleep. He has his hands together and is praying. Where is his mind? Does he know what is going on? Does he know that he might not get better? Does he see things we don't see while he has his eyes closed? Is there a path? He looks good this morning. He's on oxygen and has good color. We'll give him a breathing treatment today. He sleeps away most of the day but at 2 p.m., when the nurses are here, we have him sit up and dangle his legs off the side of the bed, lowering the bed so his toes touch the floor. He is very shaky, but that subsides and he is almost sitting up alone. He is amazed that he can do that! After we get him settled back in the bed, I notice he is doing leg lifts, which he hasn't done for a while. I remind him that I am writing a book but I need his help. "I need you to tell me some stories about you and Mom. Tell me what you did or what stands out in your mind." He is looking at me then, or through me, and I haven't gotten through to him. He can't remember, so he closes his eyes. Maybe tomorrow, Dad.

Tuesday, March 5th

I took my brother to the airport last night. I hate to have him go as it's hard to make decisions without him here, without his presence. Dad enjoys breakfast. He stares into space. I ask what he's thinking.

"I was wondering if I could make that basket." I guess the light over the big screen TV resembles a basketball hoop.

"Is it a new year yet?"

"I wish it were, Dad. I'm not liking this one too much."

MOM

Sunday, March 3rd

Alan visits her. She is calm.

Monday, March 4th

I am getting ready to call her doctor to prescribe something so we can keep Mom at Memory Lane. Alan and I set up an appointment with the powers that be at Memory Lane and we have a meeting. It's not as bad as I expected. They say they have observed her over this past week and really want to help her. They say Mom is in a living hell and doesn't want to be there. She needs to be evaluated by a geriatric neurologist, and possibly put on hospice as she has "failure to thrive" with her weight loss, not eating, and downward spiral. I ask how she's been the last two days, that it might just have been sleep deprivation and we gave her a sleeping pill so she could catch up on her sleep. Then

I listened to myself. I was making excuses to explain her actions, just like I've always done. Enough. It's not working. I will follow their advice and get her help before she ends up in a psych ward with no way out. Mom does need help in coping and I can't give it to her. I will see if I can find her the help before it is too late.

Tuesday, March 5th

I head over to Mom's for lunch and find an aide seating her at her usual table. "Asshole," she swears at the girl. Oh great, we're in for another great day. Luckily, I have Mom's word search book with me, so I say hi and present her with the book. She gets mad that someone has written all over the cover and I try to explain that's the decoration. I open the book to some pages she's already done, as I don't have a pen for her to really do some and I'm not sure she remembers how. We start on the words and she obsesses, repeating the phrases over and over and over. We find the words in the letter jumble and she starts to catch on. Lunch comes and I ask for some soup for me. It's her favorite, tomato, but she won't touch it. I tell her that's what she ordered, but she'll have nothing to do with it. A stuffed pepper, green beans, and mashed potatoes come and she refuses, and keeps obsessing about the word book that I've put away, chanting over and over again, getting loud, telling me there's a man being mean to her. He doesn't like her and he's mean. I go to her room and get a sleeping pill. I don't know how else to calm her. I text Michael to find out if the doctor has prescribed anything. I go home and call a geriatric neurologist I know and get an appointment for Mom. I am exhausted.

DAD

Wednesday, March 6th

Dad wakes up and has a good breakfast: a soft-boiled egg, applesauce with his pills, some coffee. His friend from Wisconsin calls and they chat a little. Then his friend from bridge comes over, bringing a crossword puzzle book. She says everyone at bridge misses him so when he's able to get up to the couch, we'll put up a card table and have a bridge game. After she leaves, he goes to sleep; he's made quite the effort and it's worn him out. The nurses come at noon to change and bathe him. He gets a shave, his teeth brushed, creamed arms and legs. His legs are really looking good, but I need to give him a pedicure. Michael goes out to move the cars and glimpses one of the nurses crying. Not a good sign. I had wanted Dad to try to sit up again but they said he's just too tired. It was a workout with rolling him side to side to change the sheets and change his shirt. He sleeps a lot of the afternoon, but awakens for dinnertime. I have a glass of wine, so I fix him some and we watch the news. *Wheel of Fortune* comes on while he's eating—carrots, rice and hamburger, corn pudding, and a glass of milk. I ask him if he wants a Tylenol as he seems to be a little achy. He says he's fine. He hands me his glasses, but they're not really there. We've been through this before, the imaginary things in his hands, the hand jerking. He closes his eyes.

We notice his hands aren't twitching anymore. The oxygen machine is working, but Dad is cold. Good-bye, Dad. I kiss his forehead and unfold his fingers to hold his hand. It is warm. I hold his hand for an hour. The paramedics come to pronounce him dead. Hospice comes. The sheriff comes. The funeral home reps come.

Was your Dad a World War II vet?"

"Yes," I reply.

"I saw the decal on your glass door. We can arrange a military salute with taps, and present you with a flag."

I decide I can stay and watch while Dad is moved to the stretcher, and the deep red cocoon encompasses him. Good-bye, Dad. Thanks for making me strong. Thanks for ninety-four years.

MOM

—◆◆◆—

Thursday, March 7th

My friend meets me at Memory Lane and we go in to get Mom. I don't think I'm able to handle her by myself anymore and Michael might be the man she thinks is mean to her. He is so exasperated by her. We can't find Mom, then I hear screaming from the communal bathroom. It's shower day and she is not happy. I don't know why she can't take a shower in her own bathroom. She comes out, head hung low, looking at the floor. I say, "Hi, Mom," and she perks up. I have her coat and watch, so she puts on her watch and we get the coat on and head out the door, although she is objecting, saying we can't leave, saying it's too far to walk. Where are we going? How far? We get into the car and she starts jabbering, reading all the signs along the highway. We reach the doctor's office and go inside and I start filling out her paperwork. I show her the first page to check over and give her something to do. We turn in the paperwork, and she starts watching people come into the waiting area and she alludes to the fact she's going to testify about someone who is guilty and they should go to jail.

"What are you going to say, Mom?" I ask.

"I can't tell you." She keeps going on and on about what she's going to say, and "they" might tell the truth but only "they" will know if it's the truth. We go in to see the doctor and she thinks he's the judge.

"What do you know?" she asks.

The doctor says "What should I know?"

They banter back and forth with Mom going on and on and then she gets herself so worked up she is exhausted and falls asleep. While she sleeps, the doctor gets Mom's history from me. With eyes closed, Mom starts talking, "Please come save me." She starts to indicate some head pain, then thirst and asks for water. My friend gives her a bottle of water.

"Where were you born?" the doctor asks.

She can't quite answer but turns the question around to him. They repartee for a while and then he asks, "Are you married?"

"Yes, but he's been sick for a month."

"Do you have any children?"

"Yes."

"How many?"

"One."

"What is your child's name?"

Mom thinks and comes up with "Noel." My friend and I look at each other and she mouths that it's an anagram for "Alan." I have been forgotten. The doctor tries some hand-eye coordination and reflexes. She does fine, but does try to kick him. They have a game going and she is enjoying it. She likes the attention. We leave. I have a funeral to plan. I don't tell Mom; she is in a happy place right now and I don't want to disturb it.

Walter Ephriam Schlessman Junior. Most People knew him as Walt. I knew him as Dad.

He was a hard worker, 8 to 6, six days a week for many years. When we were kids one of the high points of the day was running down to the bottom of the hill at home and jumping on the running boards of his Chevy delivery truck, then cruising up hanging on for dear life.

We had great camping trips through the years, often going to Louis Lake in Wyoming. I'm sure that was a large part of what instilled my love of the outdoors, eventually leading me back to the Rockies.

Mom and Dad were great travelers too, and growing up we took many a road trip in the station wagon, to the New York World's Fair and New England, stopping off to see Cal and Jo in Glens Falls, New York. We'd visit Grandma Cotton in Alton, Illinois, and Walt Senior and everyone in Savannah.

When we were older, Mike, Libby, and I joined Mom and Dad on our great driving tour of Europe, a wonderful introduction to the culture and food we'd only read about before. When Terri and I had our own kids, we got to cruise Alaska with the grandparents, a very memorable trip for all.

Of course it wasn't just the traveling. Many a weekend night, Dad and I would head to the local Sinclair station. He'd put the car on the hoist, but mostly it was about catching up on the local news around town.

Dad was interested in making Casper a better place. As a part of this, he was involved in the church vestry and the Shrine Club. For years we'd have Shrine Bingo Night with a giant potluck. It was always fun, even when the numbers weren't going our way.

Dad was in the Lion's Club too, becoming local president. They sponsored a summer camp on Casper Mountain for blind children. We always went to their show at the end of the season, where they could proudly display what they'd learned. When I was in high school I also got to drive the delivery truck on the hairpin turns up to the camp, taking huge boxes of groceries to the kids.

Working at the Grant Street Grocery, I was able to see Dad in action, helping his customers, organizing the staff, and making himself a financial success. I also remember the dreaded annual inventory, when Libby and I were drafted to count cans, boxes, and anything that wasn't nailed down. It was truly a family business.

The golf, well, that was Dad. He was happiest out on the course. When he'd gotten the Grant Street Grocery running like he wanted, he was able to sneak away for Wednesday afternoon outings, as well as the weekend foursomes. He was the club champion at Diamondhead, and he was well into his eighties before I had a fair chance of beating him.

Mostly, Dad taught by example: to work hard, be a member of the community, to be honest, and to love your family.

I'll miss you, Dad.

Alan

From: Dennis Bentson (dennisbentson@gmail.com)
To: mbentson@bellsouth.net
Date: Mon, March 24, 2013 1:11:31 PM
Subject: eulogy

So I woke up this morning knowing I had a lot to say about Bapa, but not knowing exactly what I was GOING to say. That's when I came to the realization that I had run out of time, much like I've run out of time with Bapa. But you and I get to have all of the wonderful times and memories that Bapa gave us. He was a man who was always happy, always thoughtful, and always caring. Looking back, I recognize that for a man to act the way Bapa did with everyone he met, he was truly happy. Incredibly happy with the love of his life With his son and daughter. With his brother. With all of his grandchildren. His GREAT grandchildren. He loved all of his family AND his friends. He loved his golf and his martinis. Both of which I learned from him to enjoy properly. I grew up getting the olives from Bapa's martinis. And when I came of age, he shared with me his philosophy on them. You can have ONE anytime. Two should be all that you have in public. Three should only be consumed in the privacy of your own home. Any more than that is a waste—since you won't remember how good the fourth one was. In playing golf with him, I learned to enjoy the moment, to not take it too seriously. But if you're going to take it seriously, play by the rules. You're only cheating yourself if you cheat. Turned out this was a good lesson for life, not just golf. I think that we can see by the size and diversity of people gathered here to celebrate Bapa's life, that he was a unique and special individual. He will be missed, but we will all live for the rest of our days knowing that he made all of our lives better just by knowing him. Thank you for everything, Bapa. All the golf, all the martinis, all the dinners and overnight stays and trips to the Diamondhead Dairy Queen where I begged you for quarters to go play the arcades. I pray that I can be some semblance of the husband, the father, the brother…the great MAN you were and are. God speed and please keep an eye out for all of us. Knowing the people in this crowd, we're all going to need a little of your luck coming down.

Denny

Wow. Thank you all for being here to join in the celebration of my Dad's Wonderful ninety-four years of life. And that's what is so great about him—every day was wonderful. I learned so much from him—truth, honesty, unconditional love, and gratefulness for each day that is given to me. He and Dr. Seuss shared the same birthdate, March 2nd. Dad was my hero, but I share with you the wisdom of Dr. Seuss: "Don't cry because it is over, smile because it happened."

Libby